Choice and Demand

Choice and Demand

PETER J. SIMMONS

Lecturer in Economics, University of Southampton

Macmillan

First published 1974 by
THE MACMILLAN PRESS LTD
London and Basingstoke
Associated companies in New York Dublin
Melbourne Johannesburg and Madras

SBN 333 15513 0 (hard cover)
333 12699 8 (paper cover)

Printed in Great Britain by
THE ANCHOR PRESS LTD
Tiptree, Essex

c c

Contents

Acknowledgements

What follows is not original but is an attempt to guide the student through the extensive and often highly mathematical body of knowledge constituting contemporary consumer theory. As such there are enormous debts to both the published literature – the most blatant of which I have tried to acknowledge in references – and to my teachers and colleagues. For the former I would like to urge all serious students to consult at least those references marked with an asterisk. The latter are primarily expressed here: to Professors Gorman, Pearce and Wise I owe a tremendous amount in both detail and perspective. To all my colleagues at Southampton I am extremely grateful for opportunities for discussion; in particular Alan Ingham, David Pearce, Ivor Pearce and Peter Saunders who read and commented on the text. The text was written before the appearance of Professor Green's book aimed at a similar audience [30]. I have since tried to revise this text to serve a largely complementary purpose to his book. Of course in the last instance the reader must judge whether or not this has been successful. The only mathematical prerequisite is calculus, though at one stage, largely for notational simplicity only, matrix algebra is used. Needless to say, I alone am responsible for omissions, misrepresentation, miscomprehensions and any other category of errors.

P. J. S.

1 Introduction

The primary purpose of economic theory is to develop a theoretical framework within which the behaviour of economic agents can be predicted in certain circumstances. The predictions are of two essentially different kinds: first, in a given situation we may, on the basis of our theory, predict that the economic agent will increase or decrease his transactions in a particular good. This is a *qualitative* prediction, since we forecast the direction of change of an activity but do not attempt to provide any numerical estimate of the amount by which the activity will change. Second, if we do make some numerical estimate then we are making a *quantitative* prediction. It is the aim of economic theory to make both kinds of predictions, but to make quantitative forecasts we obviously require a much more detailed theoretical framework than is necessary to predict directions of change. Traditional demand theory contented itself largely with qualitative conclusions, and it is only comparatively recently that the development of econometrics has made quantitative forecasts possible.

It is obvious, then, that the first task of the economist is to construct a theoretical framework in terms of which the behaviour of producers and consumers can be discussed. Any such theory must involve certain basic *axioms* or assumptions which lay down the kind of conceptual world with which the theory is concerned. The axioms themselves are accepted as basic truths within which the theory must be developed; hence it is rather important that we should carefully select an axiomatic system with some claim of relevance to the real social phenomena we are trying to analyse. In a general sense, as its basic framework, economic theory is concerned with the production of goods from resources by producers, and the allocation of goods between consumers through some kind of exchange mechanism. By making each of these concepts more precise the economist can construct a *general equilibrium* theory, stressing the interdependence of the mechanisms at work in the markets for different goods.

However, demand theory is a *partial equilibrium* theory dealing only with a small part of the problems of production and allocation. Indeed, even then, traditional demand theory can be applied only to rather special circumstances. First, let us only consider economies in which the exchange of goods is performed through a price mechanism. There is one good which serves as a unit of account (money) and each other good has a price expressed in terms of this unit of account. Second, consumers are assumed to own all the resources, which they either sell or hire out to producers for the purpose of production, receiving in exchange a sum of money. It is only in these special kinds of economy, typified as *market mechanism private ownership economies,* and only at this stage of the economic process that traditional demand theory assumes a central role. Each consumer has a certain money income and faces certain market prices for each of the goods that he could buy. It is the purpose of demand theory to provide a theoretical framework within which we can analyse the purchases of goods which the consumer chooses to make. The theory proceeds to make qualitative and, with the aid of econometrics, some quantitative predictions of how the consumer will change his purchases of goods if the market situation that he is facing changes.

Demand theory can be said to represent directly the actual functioning of the economic system only in these types of economies. Nevertheless it is extremely relevant to the economic processes of Western society since Western society is largely characterised by this type of economic structure. Moreover demand theory is not necessarily irrelevant even if there is no market mechanism. Consider, as a second case, a centrally planned economy in which each individual is allocated a ration of every good and is ordered to supply a definite quantity of each resource in a consistent fashion: i.e. total use of each good is equal to total supply. Then, although there are no explicit market prices, we may still identify a system of implicit *shadow prices* which reflect the scarcity of each good and which would have led, under perfect competition, to the given allocations. Furthermore if we wish to assess the functioning of such an economy from a normative viewpoint, it is difficult to see how this could be done without taking some account of individual consumer preferences, which form the core of traditional demand theory.

The predictions made may be of a *comparative static* nature: telling us, for example, that if the market price of one of the goods changes and if the consumer has optimally adjusted his purchases how his consumption pattern will differ between the two optimal positions. Note that in order for this problem to be well defined there must exist a unique optimum position both before and after the change in the particular parameter. On the other hand we may construct models of *dynamic* consumer behaviour, predicting the time path that will be followed by the purchases of the consumer as he adjusts to any change gradually over time.

As a preliminary we should explicitly define the notion of a consumer. For the purposes of what follows, a consumer is any individual who is faced with the problem of allocating a stock of purchasing power, at a given instant of time, between a variety of alternative options available to him. Thus a firm wishing to choose its purchases of factors of production may, in some contexts, be treated as a consumer.

Finally we should stress that much of what follows is not the most general theory possible. Extensive use is made of calculus – even in situations where, strictly speaking, it is not justified – because this is still more familiar to most students than the more modern set-theoretic approaches. Similarly the axioms within which we work are much more stringent than is necessary to develop a consistent body of consumer theory.

2 The Preference Structure of the Individual and the Theory of Demand

THE AXIOM SYSTEM

Demand theory aims to analyse the choices that individuals make between the goods and services that are available to them.

To proceed with this aim, we have to define the concepts used to represent the objects to be purchased and to represent the wishes of the consumer for possessing those objects and express the rules the consumer adopts, possibly unconsciously, for making his choices. A good can be defined as any tangible or intangible object which any individual in society may conceivably wish to acquire or use under some circumstances, or which any consumer cannot help acquiring under some conceivable circumstances. Note that this definition includes not only objects such as various foodstuffs but also intangible objects such as atmospheric pollution. At this level of generality the goods which the consumer could purchase can be interpreted to include both current consumption goods and consumer durables, or consumption goods which, though paid for now, will not be received or consumed until some date in the future [17]. An example might be payment now for a pound of tea of a particular quality to be consumed in a particular place in five years' time. We may then, if we wish, interpret the consumer's purchasing pattern as fixing the consumption of each good available at every instant over his lifetime. The essential point is that by regarding a physically identical commodity purchased now in a given situation for use at two different times or two different places as two distinct economic goods we can use the choice framework to allow the consumer to determine now his whole lifetime pattern of consumption. If we do so then the number of goods is likely to be very large, but, if we treat time and place in a discrete fashion, still finite. In summary then, different goods are distinct either in their physical composition or their availability, but different units of the same good are sufficiently homogeneous, for it to be sensible to define the quantity of a good by a number of units of that good. We suppose that there is some finite number of n goods amongst which choices must be made, and that each good is available in any finite non-negative quantity. This implies that all goods are divisible, whereas we know in reality that this is not the case. Nevertheless to make this assumption considerably simplifies the task of developing the theory, since we can appeal to the techniques of calculus which require us to deal with very small magnitudes of change. Also, as we proceed, the means of dealing with indivisibilities should become evident. A *commodity bundle* consists of a definite non-negative quantity of each of the goods, so that if x_i represents the quantity of the ith good then a commodity bundle containing n goods is represented by a list $\mathbf{x} = (x_1 \ldots x_n)$. The list $\mathbf{x}$ will be referred to as a *vector*: with two or three goods it may be interpreted as a point in two- or three-dimensional space. With an arbitrary finite number n of goods we can imagine $\mathbf{x}$ as a point in n-dimensional space: i.e. a space which has n axes. There is assumed to be a definite collection X of all the commodity bundles which the consumer could choose, and we shall think of X as the whole of the non-negative region of the n-dimensional space. The problem facing the consumer is to choose points from X according to his tastes. To express this notion, we suppose that the consumer is capable of ordering all the commodity bundles in X in such a way that bundles coming higher in the ordering would be chosen by the consumer over bundles coming lower in the ordering of the consumer in situations where both bundles were available. To express this more formally, if $\mathbf{x}$ and $\mathbf{y}$ are any two commodity bundles, let us define $\mathbf{x}R\mathbf{y}$ to mean that the bundle $\mathbf{x}$ is at least as desirable as the bundle $\mathbf{y}$ in the eyes of the consumer. The notion of a preference ordering R over all available commodity bundles X is the basic conceptual element required to construct a theory of preferences: the theory proceeds by laying down axioms on the ordering R which are designed to enable us to prove that any consumer satisfying our axioms would make his choices in such a way that his choice behaviour would be indistinguishable from that of a consumer who possessed a *utility function* with certain desirable properties. We shall first list the axioms and then discuss them.

Axiom 1: The Axiom of Completeness. The consumer has an ordering relation R such that for any two bundles $\mathbf{x}$, $\mathbf{y}$ in X either $\mathbf{x}R\mathbf{y}$ or $\mathbf{y}R\mathbf{x}$ or both hold.

Axiom 2: The Axiom of Transitivity. The relation R is *transitive*, so that for any bundles $\mathbf{x}$, $\mathbf{y}$, $\mathbf{z}$ in X if $\mathbf{x}R\mathbf{y}$ and $\mathbf{y}R\mathbf{z}$ then it must be true that $\mathbf{x}R\mathbf{z}$.

To introduce our third axiom, recall the meaning of vector inequalities: $\mathbf{x} \geqslant \mathbf{y}$ means that, for all $i = 1 \ldots n$, $x_i \geqslant y_i$ and, for at least one value of i, $x_i > y_i$. In words, $\mathbf{x}$ must be at least as great as $\mathbf{y}$ in each of its components and must be actually greater than $\mathbf{y}$ in at least one component. Our third axiom is commonly referred to as an axiom of greed, for obvious reasons:

Axiom 3: The Axiom of Greed. For any two bundles $\mathbf{x}$ and $\mathbf{y}$ in X if $\mathbf{x} \geqslant \mathbf{y}$ then it must be true that $\mathbf{x}R\mathbf{y}$ and not $\mathbf{y}R\mathbf{x}$ both hold.

Axiom 4: The Axiom of Continuity. For any two bundles $\mathbf{x}$ and $\mathbf{y}$ in X if $\mathbf{x}P\mathbf{y}$ then it is possible to find a small region of bundles $\mathbf{z}$ in X entirely surrounding $\mathbf{y}$ so that for any such bundle $\mathbf{z}$ it must be true that $\mathbf{x}P\mathbf{z}$. In words, this axiom states that bundles which are close together in a numerical sense must also be close together in the sense of the ordering.

Axiom 5: The Axiom of Convexity. If $\mathbf{x}$, $\mathbf{y}$ and $\mathbf{z}$ are any three bundles in X such that $\mathbf{y}R\mathbf{x}$ and $\mathbf{z}R\mathbf{x}$ both hold then for any number λ, $0 \leqslant \lambda \leqslant 1$, it must be true that $[\lambda\mathbf{y} + (1 - \lambda)\mathbf{z}]R\mathbf{x}$.

The first axiom tells us that for any pair of bundles at all that could be made available to the individual, the individual knows his own mind sufficiently to be able to order the bundles under R. This must mean that either the individual has some experience of all goods so that he is capable of judging the advantages and disadvantages of all bundles, or that he has some rule of thumb for deciding his preferences between bundles of which he has no experience. An implicit assumption underlying the axiom is that the preferences of the individual do not depend on which bundles he is asked to compare or on the nature of the collection X. Exogenous forces such as advertising or wider social phenomena may play their role in shaping the preferences of the individual, but at any instant of time, faced with some collection X, the preference ordering can be taken as a given factor. The axiom is innocuous in that it is clearly a necessary condition for choice between any two commodity bundles available to be possible. We can define notions of *indifference* and of *strict preference* as orderings derived from the ordering R in an intuitively satisfying fashion: thus for any two bundles **x**, **y** in X **x** is indifferent to **y** (written **x**I**y**) if and only if **x**R**y** and **y**R**x** both hold. Similarly for any two bundles **x** and **y** in X, **x** is strictly preferred to **y** (written as **x**P**y**), if and only if both **x**R**y** and not **y**R**x** hold. In terms of the indifference ordering I, the problem of constructing a preference ordering for the individual is essentially that of finding the weakest restrictions on R which will endow the consumer with indifference classes (i.e. collections of bundles any two of which are indifferent to one another) which exactly resemble the traditional indifference curves.

An implicit statement of the properties of I is embodied in the first axiom. The axiom contains no restriction that the two bundles should be distinct; if in fact we take the case where **x** = **y**, then the axiom yields that for all **x** in X, **x**R**x** which in its turn implies for all **x** in X, **x**I**x**. It is an entirely reasonable assertion to suppose that every bundle in X should be indifferent to itself. Similarly it is reasonable to suppose that every bundle is at least as desirable as itself. This is referred to as the condition of '*reflexiveness*'.

The second axiom is designed to eliminate the possibility of cycles in the ordering of the consumer so that 'loops' of the form **x**R**y**, **y**R**z**, **z**R**x** are excluded. If such 'loops' did exist then our interpretation of R as meaning 'at least as desirable as' would force us to conclude that the individual had a preference ordering involving contradictory rankings. Thus if transitivity broke down we would be faced with a situation where simultaneously the individual considered **x** as at least as desirable as

z and also **x** as not at least as desirable as **z**. As an axiom of consistency this again appears to be an innocuous assumption. Consider the circumstances under which it may fail to hold. As Newman [45] and Georgescu-Roegen [25] have pointed out, if there is a 'threshold of perception' in the mind of the consumer so that bundles can only be ordered when there is a perceptible and sufficiently large difference between them, then the individual might be unable to distinguish between **x** and **y** and between **y** and **z** and yet be able to distinguish between **x** and **z** on the basis of a greater physical difference between the bundles. This could lead to the pattern **x**R**y**, **y**R**z** and **z**P**x**. A further case in which transitivity may break down arises when preferences between goods are based on several criteria. A celebrated illustration has been provided by Allais [1], where the choice is between gambles, and the two criteria are presumably the average return expected from the gamble and the riskiness attached to the gamble. A further example is given by May [41].

There is another way of looking at the transitivity condition which is quite instructive. In a two-dimensional illustration (Fig. 1) suppose that **x**P**y**, for two bundles **x**, **y**. Then if we find all bundles **z** such that **x**R**z** we could delineate a collection of bundles like, for example, the horizontally shaded collection in the diagram. Similarly we can find all bundles **z** such that **y**R**z**, as might be represented by the vertically shaded collection. Then the transitivity axiom tells us that this set of bundles for **y** must be entirely contained within this set of bundles for **x**. In slightly more formal language, if we refer to these collections of bundles as the *inferior set* connected with **x** or **y**, then the transitivity axiom means that for any **x** and **y** if **x**R**y** then the inferior set of **y** is entirely contained within the inferior set of **x**. Inferior sets corresponding to different bundles are nested within one another so that the transitivity axiom leads from a statement of ordering of two given bundles to a certain consistency in the ordering relations between all bundles lower in the ordering than the two given bundles.

The greed axiom has intuitively clear content. Cases can easily be thought of which violate the axiom: for example the individual may be completely indifferent to a good in any quantity in the way that a teetotaller might be completely indifferent to the quantity of alcohol included in a commodity bundle. Even if we allow for the fact that the teetotaller experiences some inconvenience in disposing of the alcohol this would presumably be reflected in the teetotaller preferring bundles with a smaller quantity of alcohol to those with a larger quantity. Since we have restricted our bundles to have

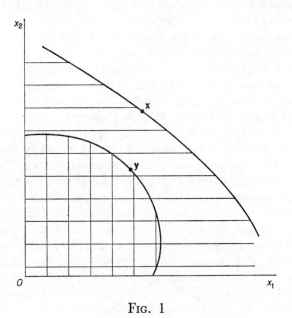

Fig. 1

all components non-negative the usual device of changing the definition of a good to measure the good negatively rather than positively and so continue to satisfy the greed axiom is not available to us. We have to conclude that the greed axiom is a severe restriction on the relevance of the theory since it requires that the individual should nowhere be *satiated* with respect to any good for any bundle in the collection X.

The fourth axiom is a statement that the preference ordering should be continuous and that no wide jumps in the ordering are possible. If two commodity bundles are physically close together then they must not be widely apart in the ordering.

This axiom is really only necessary because we are insisting that there is a non-finite collection of commodity bundles over which the consumer is required to express his preferences. It is easy to see that if there are only a finite number of bundles to be ordered $(\mathbf{x}_1, \mathbf{x}_2 \ldots \mathbf{x}_n)$ transitively then it is straightforward to define a *utility function* representing preferences. Thus if we assign the number n to the bundle highest in the ordering; $(n-1)$ to the next highest bundle and so on with the lowest bundle being assigned a value of 1 then we have defined a utility function $u(\mathbf{x})$ such that $u(\mathbf{x}_i) \geqslant u(\mathbf{x}_j)$ if and only if $\mathbf{x}_i R \mathbf{x}_j$. To illustrate the axiom, suppose that we have a fixed bundle $\mathbf{y}$ in X and a never-ending sequence or list of bundles $\mathbf{x}_1, \mathbf{x}_2 \ldots \mathbf{x}_n \ldots$ each of which is in X and such that, for each term $\mathbf{x}_i$ in the list, $\mathbf{x}_i R \mathbf{y}$. Suppose also that the sequence of bundles $\mathbf{x}_i$ gets gradually closer and closer to some particular bundle $\mathbf{x}$; then the axiom of continuity states that it must be true that $\mathbf{x} R \mathbf{y}$. In other words, if, for all $\mathbf{x}_i$, $\mathbf{x}_i R \mathbf{y}$ then it is impossible to suddenly switch to $\mathbf{y} P \mathbf{x}$ (i.e. to not $\mathbf{x} R \mathbf{y}$) without moving through some commodity bundle $\mathbf{x}^*$ which is indifferent to $\mathbf{y}$. The axiom is a restriction on the way in which preferences between close pairs of bundles are related and it imposes a certain regular 'smoothness' on the individual's ordering. Again the axiom is a fairly severe restriction on the nature of preference, and one can imagine cases where the axiom does not hold. Well-known examples are those of a *lexicographic ordering* [19] [45] [25]. Here tastes between two bundles are defined first by the quantity of the first good, so that if $\mathbf{x}$, $\mathbf{y}$ are such that $x_1 > y_1$ then $\mathbf{x} P \mathbf{y}$, regardless of quantities of the other goods. If $x_1 = y_1$ but $x_2 > y_2$ then again $\mathbf{x} P \mathbf{y}$; the ordering between $\mathbf{x}$ and $\mathbf{y}$ proceeds in this way through all n components of the bundles, with earlier components having priority over later components in defining the ordering. This case does not satisfy the continuity axiom: in Fig. 2, $\mathbf{x} R \mathbf{y}$ since $x_1 = y_1$ but $x_2 > y_2$, whereas points like $\mathbf{z}$ which are indefinitely close to $\mathbf{x}$ are strictly inferior to $\mathbf{y}$ since they contain less of the first good.

Axiom 5, the convexity axiom, states that averages of bundles at least as desirable as a given bundle are themselves at least as desirable as the given bundle. This axiom may be interpreted as stating that 'variety is the spice of life' or, alternatively, the

more one has of a good the less will one desire further incre-
ments in the good. Again this is a definite restriction on the
type of consumer with which we are concerned; nevertheless
we shall see later that if the individual is purchasing bundles
according to his preference ordering at every instant of time,
and if we only observe his average daily behaviour then the

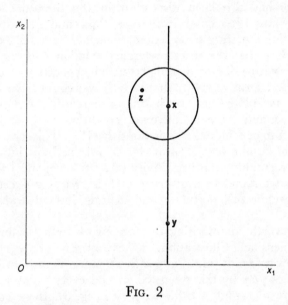

FIG. 2

observable implications of his behaviour with or without this
axiom may well be the same.

On the basis of this axiom system we can already deduce quite
a lot about the individual and his preferences. We could start
by considering the relations between the orderings R, I and P
assuming always that axioms 1 and 2 hold. It is then immediate
from the definitions of I and P that

(1) I is transitive
(2) $\mathbf{x}I\mathbf{y}$ if and only if $\mathbf{y}I\mathbf{x}$
(3) If $\mathbf{x}P\mathbf{y}$ then it is not true that $\mathbf{y}P\mathbf{x}$
(4) P is transitive.

To demonstrate the kinds of argument involved we shall show
that P is transitive. Let $\mathbf{x}P\mathbf{y}$ and $\mathbf{y}P\mathbf{z}$. Then we must show that

$\mathbf{x}R\mathbf{z}$ and not $\mathbf{z}R\mathbf{x}$ both hold. By transitivity of R, the first of these is obvious. To show the second, suppose that the conclusion is false and then show that such a supposition leads to a contradiction: thus let $\mathbf{z}R\mathbf{x}$. Then since $\mathbf{x}P\mathbf{y}$ we deduce that $\mathbf{z}R\mathbf{y}$ by transitivity of R, which contradicts the premise that $\mathbf{y}P\mathbf{z}$.

There has also been discussion in the literature of the relationships between transitivity of R, I and P. Instead of postulating our transitivity axiom, we could have started from a postulate that the strict preference relation P is transitive, together with a slightly modified convexity condition, to deduce that R is transitive [60]. Alternatively we could have started from a postulate that the indifference relation I should be transitive and have a convexity condition very similar to Axiom 5 to conclude that R is transitive [57]. This seems to be quite important since transitivity of I is perhaps intuitively more acceptable than transitivity of R: the weight of the objections we found to transitivity of R is greatly reduced once we abandon this postulate and assume instead transitivity of I.

It is worth summarising the framework by appealing to a two-dimensional illustration. Take any $\mathbf{x} = (x_1, x_2)$ in X. Then, every point $\mathbf{y}$ in the 'positive quadrant' with 'origin' at $\mathbf{x}$ satisfies $\mathbf{y}R\mathbf{x}$ by the greed axiom and every point $\mathbf{y}$ in the 'negative quadrant' satisfies $\mathbf{x}R\mathbf{y}$ (see Fig. 3). If we consider all bundles $\mathbf{y}$ such that $\mathbf{y}I\mathbf{x}$ then since, by the greed axiom, two bundles can only be indifferent if whenever one contains more of one good than the other it also contains less of some other good, this locus must be downward sloping from left to right so long as points distinct from $\mathbf{x}$ but indifferent to $\mathbf{x}$ exist. By the continuity axiom, we know that as we move down any positively sloping straight line, such as AB in Fig. 3, from points in the 'positive quadrant' to points in the 'negative quadrant' we must pass through some point $\mathbf{y}^*$ such that $\mathbf{y}^*I\mathbf{x}$ and hence elements indifferent to, but distinct from, $\mathbf{x}$ exist. By the transitivity axiom we know that loci of bundles indifferent to different bundles $\mathbf{x}$ lying on a positively sloped line can never touch or intersect. Again by the greed axiom, we know that the loci of bundles indifferent to a fixed $\mathbf{x}$ must be

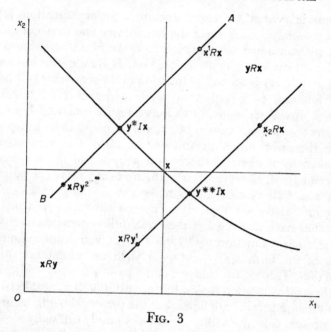

FIG. 3

'thin' curves and can contain no *band* of bundles indifferent to one another. Finally, by the convexity axiom these loci must either be straight lines or must be convex to the origin or may have segments of both types.

CONSUMER EQUILIBRIUM

It is clear that we have a map of 'indifference loci' defined by the logical ordering I to all intents and purposes identical with the customary indifference map. It will not be surprising to learn that we can in fact find a continuous utility function which represents the preference ordering R in the sense that $\mathbf{x}R\mathbf{y}$ if and only if $u(x_1 \ldots x_n) \geqslant u(y_1 \ldots y_n)$ where $u(.)$ is the utility function. Moreover the utility function will satisfy all the properties which ensure that the map of indifference curves corresponding to the utility function will look exactly like our 'indifference loci'. Hence with any consumer who satisfies our axiomatic system we can associate a utility function [19]. This is merely a convenient analytic device and does not mean that the consumer has explicitly to make his choice according to the utility function we assign him. It should also be noted that $u(x_1 \ldots x_n)$ is an *ordinal* function in the sense that, if $F(u)$ is any function of u such that $u_1 > u_2$ implies $F(u_1) > F(u_2)$, then $F(u)$ will serve just as well as a utility function. For consumers obeying our system of axioms we could in fact dispense with the utility function and deduce all of the conventional conclusions of demand theory solely by use of the preference ordering itself. However, it is mathematically more convenient, and also follows custom, to make use of the ordinal utility function. Later we shall discuss some situations in which it becomes natural to assign a *cardinal* utility function to a consumer: i.e. a function $u(x)$ such that only transformations of $u(x)$ of the form $v(x) = au(x) + b$ yield an acceptable utility function. This means that we can choose the scale and origin of the utility function freely, but the utility differences between bundles are precisely defined. For the present though, it should be stressed that the utility function is purely ordinal.

To derive the results of traditional demand theory we must now put the individual in a market situation possessing a fixed money income M and facing fixed market prices for the goods $\mathbf{p} = (p_1, p_2 \ldots p_n)$. Note that in assuming fixed prices we are assuming *perfect competition* amongst consumers, since the individual consumer is taken to be incapable of affecting market prices through his actions.

We should also note that the interpretation of both M and p_i depends on our definition and treatment of goods. Thus if some goods include physical commodities purchased now for receipt in the future, then the price of these goods is the price which would be observed on a futures market in the physical commodity. If consumer choices determine the consumer's whole lifetime pattern of consumption, then the variable M has the natural economic interpretation of the present value of consumer's wealth; it includes initial assets of the consumer and all discounted future income flows to the consumer. On the other hand, if we wish to define goods as purely current consumption goods then the variable M could be defined as total current consumption expenditure. This in turn might be defined as either current money income minus current savings, or the present value of wealth minus the part of the present value of wealth which is transferred into the future for expenditure on future consumption goods. Since the utility function reflects the tastes of the individual we can describe the individual's market behaviour by the solution to the problem

$$\text{Maximise } u(x_1, x_2 \ldots x_n)$$

over all $x_1 \ldots x_n$ which satisfy

$$\sum_{i=1}^{n} p_i x_i \leqslant M$$

In fact, by the greed axiom, the consumer will always be able to increase his level of utility by consuming an additional unit of one good and no less of any other, so that as long as market prices are all positive, we can always assume the individual spends all of his money income. The budget constraint then becomes

$$\sum_{i=1}^{n} p_i x_i = M.$$

It should also be noted that by placing the individual in a market situation we have narrowed the realm of discussion; so long as we were only considering the preference structure of the individual, the x's over which preferences are defined could be interpreted quite generally as anything which affects the the satisfaction of the individual. In particular some of the x's could represent consumption of goods by other individuals, or aspects of government activity [44].

However, even if this were the case, we could still represent those aspects of consumer behaviour of the private market type by holding constant at some level all factors in the utility function not of this kind and by subtracting from income in the budget constraint all expenditure not of this kind. We will then get results for private market maximisation conditional on the fixed values of the other activity. It is also true that by characterising an individual with the same preference structure in all market situations we are excluding the possibility that the preference ordering may depend on the particular market situation faced by the individual, as might occur if the quality or desirability of goods tends to be judged by their price [35]. Hence by regarding market behaviour as capable of description by the solution to the maximisation problem we are introducing some restrictions.

To solve the maximisation problem means that we find the commodity bundle $(x_1 \ldots x_n)$ which gives the highest level of

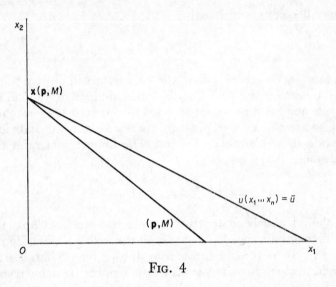

FIG. 4

utility while satisfying the budget constraint. Under our assumptions the optimising $(x_1 \ldots x_n)$ will always exist for non-negative prices and income, but since our convexity assumption allows indifference curves to be linear it may not be unique; Figs 4 and 5 illustrate the effect of linear indifference curves for two goods. When the budget line *coincides* with the highest attainable indifference curve (Fig. 5) then any $(x_1 \ldots x_n)$ on the budget line is optimal. Otherwise with linear indifference curves we may have *corner solutions* as in Fig. 4. In the main argument we shall exclude this possibility, treating it as a special case so that we generally assume there is a unique optimum for each price and income (Fig. 6). This clearly

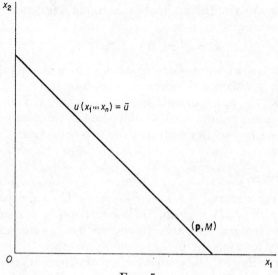

Fig. 5

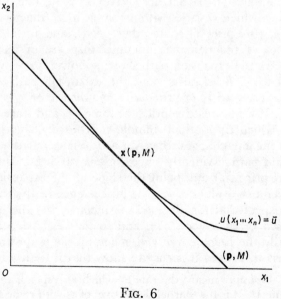

Fig. 6

allows us to write the optimal $(x_1 \ldots x_n)$ as a function of prices and incomes as

$$x_i = f^i(\mathbf{p}, M) \quad (i = 1 \ldots n)$$

in the form of a system of *demand functions*. Note that if $(x_1^* \ldots x_n^*)$ solves the problem with prices $(p_1 \ldots p_n)$ and income M, then it also solves the problem with prices $(\lambda p_1 \ldots \lambda p_n)$ and income λM where λ is any positive number, since exactly the same collection of commodity bundles $\mathbf{x}$ satisfies the two equations:

$$\sum_{i=1}^{n} p_i x_i = M \quad \text{and} \quad \sum_{i=1}^{n} (\lambda p_i) \, x_i = (\lambda M)$$

Hence the demand function $f^i(.)$ must have the particular property $f^i(\mathbf{p}, M) = f^i(\lambda \mathbf{p}, \lambda M)$ for all positive numbers λ. Since the budget constraint remains unchanged on multiplying all prices and income by any positive number λ it is obvious geometrically that the optimal $\mathbf{x}$ remains unchanged.

In order to derive the qualitative predictions of traditional demand theory we need to know much more about the demand functions $f^i(\mathbf{p}, M)$; in particular, we need to know as much as possible about the partial derivatives of these functions: i.e. the way in which x_i varies with a change in p_i (the good's own price), p_j (the price of some other good), and with M. Two properties of the demand functions that are of immediate interest are the expansion path showing how x_i varies with M, referred to as *Engel curves*; and the expansion path showing how x_i varies with p_i – the *price consumption* or *offer* curves (Fig. 7). If we fix relative prices at some p^*, and trace out the way in which the optimal bundle purchased changes as the level of income changes, then we are tracing out the income expansion path. Evidently since we are varying income with constant prices, at any point the slope of the expansion path depends on the values of $\partial x_i / \partial M$ for each good.[1] In general we might expect that for all goods as income rises the quantity purchased of each good rises and so that $\partial x_i / \partial M \geqslant 0$. Geometrically the Engel curve will generally slope upwards from left to right. Indeed it is easy to show that if we assume non-

---

[1] $\partial x_i / \partial M$ simply means the rate at which x_i responds to a small change in M. It is the 'partial derivative' of x_i with respect to M.

satiation then it cannot be true for all goods that $\partial x_i / \partial M \leqslant 0$, since whenever income increases at constant prices, the total value of expenditure must increase, and hence purchases of at least one of the goods must increase. However, for some goods, known as *inferior goods*, we may well have $\partial x_i / \partial M < 0$ so that the Engel curve in the (ij) plane may not everywhere have a positive slope. Examples of such goods might be bread: when

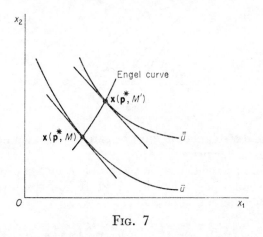

FIG. 7

income rises, cakes and biscuits may tend to be substituted for bread.

The offer curve indicates how optimal purchases vary as relative prices vary with income held constant, and hence at each point the slope of the offer curve obviously depends on the values of $\partial x_i / \partial p_j$. Thus, suppose there are only two goods (x_1, x_2) and we vary p_1 keeping p_2 and M fixed; geometrically the position is shown in Fig. 8: as the price p_1 continually falls the optimal bundle purchased moves from left to right along the offer curve. One might expect that, as the price of a good falls, more of the good is purchased; in fact a large part of traditional demand theory is concerned with investigating when this is so. It should be noted that if we have a system of demand functions with n goods, then there are many ways of allowing relative prices to vary while holding income constant, depending on the particular price, or prices, we wish to vary. Hence

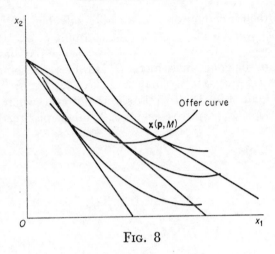

FIG. 8

any particular offer curve must be carefully defined in the context of particular price changes.

We could proceed to solve the problem by the direct use of Lagrange multipliers which would require us to solve for $(x_1^* \ldots x_n^*)$ which maximise

$$L(\mathbf{x}, \lambda) = u(x_1^* \ldots x_n) + \lambda \left(M - \sum_{i=1}^{n} p_i x_i \right)$$

over $(x_1 \ldots x_n)$ and for λ^* which equates

$$\frac{\partial L(x^*, \lambda)}{\partial \lambda} = 0 = (M - \sum p_i x_i)$$

so that the budget constraint holds. Here λ is an undetermined multiplier. Note that in order for the dimensions of this expression to be commensurate, λ must have the dimensions of 'utility per unit of income'. In fact it can be shown that λ is equal to the *marginal utility of income*; it measures the increase in utility which could be achieved from a unit increase in income, when all quantities purchased are optimally adjusted to the given budget constraint. If we do proceed to maximise the Lagrangian function with respect to the quantities consumed then if $\mathbf{x}^*$ is a maximising commodity bundle it must satisfy the equation system:

$$\frac{\partial u(\mathbf{x}^*)}{\partial x_i} = \lambda^* p_i \quad (i = 1 \ldots n)$$

$$\sum_{i=1}^{n} p_i x_i^* = M$$

In all there are $(n+1)$ equations. The first n state that the slope of the indifference curve in any plane

$$\frac{\partial u(\mathbf{x}^*)}{\partial x_i} \bigg/ \frac{\partial u(\mathbf{x}^*)}{\partial x_j}$$

should be equal, at the maximising point, to the slope of the budget line p_i/p_j so that no reallocation of expenditure among the available goods can lead to an increase in utility. Thus if

$$\frac{\partial u(\mathbf{x}^*)}{\partial x_i} \bigg/ \frac{\partial u(\mathbf{x}^*)}{\partial x_j} > \frac{p_i}{p_j}$$

then it is true that

$$\frac{p_j}{p_i} \cdot \frac{\partial u(\mathbf{x}^*)}{\partial x_i} > \frac{\partial u(\mathbf{x}^*)}{\partial x_j}$$

If the consumer purchases a unit less of x_j and spends the additional income released on good i then the additional income released is p_j while the number of units of good i which may be purchased with this income is $(1/p_i) \cdot p_j$.

In giving up a unit of good j the consumer suffers a utility loss of $\partial u(\mathbf{x}^*)/\partial x_i$, but from consuming the additional p_j/p_i units of good i, he enjoys a utility gain of $\partial u(\mathbf{x}^*)/\partial x_i$. Since

$$\frac{p_j}{p_i} \frac{\partial u(\mathbf{x}^*)}{\partial x_i} > \frac{\partial u(\mathbf{x}^*)}{\partial x_j}$$

his utility gain outweighs his utility loss. If the consumer is maximising his utility any such reallocation is impossible and this can only be so if marginal rates of substitution are equated to relative prices. The last equation in the system states merely that the budget constraint must hold. We have $(n+1)$ equations and $(n+1)$ variables $(x_1^* \ldots x_n^*, \lambda)$ so that in general we can expect to solve for each x_i, λ as functions of $(p_1 \ldots p_n, M)$. This provides the algebraic basis for the system of demand functions.

We can now easily deduce that the undetermined multiplier λ^* corresponds to the marginal utility of income. At the optimum we have

$$L(\mathbf{x}^*, \lambda^*) = u(\mathbf{x}^*) + \lambda^*(M - \sum p_i x_i^*) = u(\mathbf{x}^*)$$

where $x_i^* = x_i\,(\mathbf{p}, M)$. So

$$\frac{\mathrm{d}u(\mathbf{x}^*)}{\mathrm{d}M} = \sum_{i=1}^{n} \frac{\partial u(\mathbf{x}^*)}{\partial x_i}\ \frac{\partial x_i}{\partial M} + \lambda^* - \lambda^* \sum_{i=1}^{n} p_i \frac{\partial x_i}{\partial M}$$

$$= \sum_{i=1}^{n} \left(\frac{\partial u(\mathbf{x}^*)}{\partial x_i} - \lambda^* p_i\right) \frac{\partial x_i}{\partial M} + \lambda^* = \lambda^*$$

since the optimising quantities $\mathbf{x}^*$ ensure marginal rates of substitution are equal to price ratios.

INDIRECT UTILITY FUNCTIONS

Once we have the system of demand functions, we can use them to express the utility function as dependent on prices and incomes. We can substitute the demand functions into the utility function to deduce

$$u(x_1 \ldots x_n) = u\{x_1(\mathbf{p}, M) \ldots x_n(\mathbf{p}, M)\} = v(\mathbf{p}, M)$$

where, since all quantities demanded are unchanged with a proportional change in all prices and income, the level of utility v is also unchanged under such proportional changes. This function, known as the *indirect utility function*, is useful primarily because we can derive a simple expression for the demand functions in terms of the partial derivatives of the function $v(\mathbf{p}, M)$. In other words if we are given an arbitrary function of prices and incomes which arises in the course of some investigation, then, in order to examine whether the arbitrary function can be interpreted as a true indirect utility function, we have only to examine the relevant partial derivatives of the arbitrary function to see if they satisfy all the properties required of demand functions.

Thus, consider the effect of a price change in the *j*th good,

dp_j accompanied by an income change, δM, which is just sufficient to compensate for the price change in the sense that the level of utility remains unchanged from the simultaneous changes (dp_j, δM). Then we have

$$dv(\mathbf{p}, M) = \frac{\partial v(\mathbf{p}, M)}{\partial M} \, \delta M + \frac{\partial v(\mathbf{p}, M)}{\partial p_j} \, dp_j = 0$$

since the utility level is unchanged. However, the compensating income change is exactly equal to $x_j dp_j$ since if $\delta M = x_j \, dp_j$ then the consumer can just, but only just, afford to purchase the bundle $\mathbf{x}$ which he purchased before the price change. Hence

$$\frac{\partial v(\mathbf{p}, M)}{\partial M} \, x_j dp_j + \frac{\partial v(\mathbf{p}, M)}{\partial p_j} \, dp_j = 0$$

From which we deduce that

$$x_j = -\frac{\partial v(\mathbf{p}, M)}{\partial p_j} \Big/ \frac{\partial v(\mathbf{p}, M)}{\partial M}$$

which is a direct characterisation of the demand functions in terms of prices and income.

INCOME AND SUBSTITUTION EFFECTS

However, rather than proceed by examining the properties of the partial derivatives of the demand functions directly from the maximising conditions, we shall use a different and rather more convenient approach.

Consider first the change in demand for the ith good when the price of the jth good changes with all other prices and income held constant. This can be regarded as the sum of two movements: first, if the level of utility is held constant, then the individual will change his optimal purchases of goods in response to the change in relative prices by moving round the constant indifference curve until his new budget line is just tangential to that indifference curve; second, since a change in the price of the jth good alters the *real* purchasing power of the constant *money* income of the consumer, the consumer will shift from one indifference curve to another, changing his purchases of x_i by an amount given by his marginal propensity to consume x_i and the importance of the change in real income. To formalise these notions we will follow an argument of Yokoyama [61]. We wish to derive an expression for the way in which purchases of the ith good change as the price of the jth good changes and money income simultaneously changes in

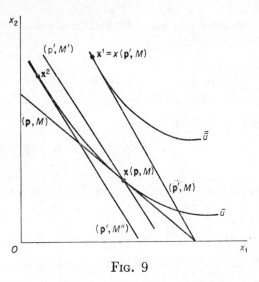

Fig. 9

such a way as to just leave the consumer on the same indifference curve as previously. But in the face of the simultaneous changes $(\varDelta p_j, \varDelta M)$ where $\varDelta M$ is the change in income just sufficient to compensate for the price change $\varDelta p_j$ in the sense that the consumer can just attain the same indifference curve; we have

$$\frac{\varDelta x_i}{\varDelta p_j}\bigg|_{\text{utility constant}} \varDelta p_j = \frac{\varDelta x_i}{\varDelta p_j} \cdot \varDelta p_j + \frac{\varDelta x_i}{\varDelta M} \cdot \varDelta M$$

In Fig. 9 we can express the shift from $\mathbf{x}$ in the original budgetary situation to $\mathbf{x}^2$ in the new budgetary situation after the simultaneous price and income changes as the sum of the shift to $\mathbf{x}^1$ due solely to the price change and then the shift from

$\mathbf{x}^1$ to $\mathbf{x}^2$ due to the income change. However, we can explicitly calculate the necessary income change as

$$\Delta M = \sum_{i=1}^{n} p_i' x^2 - \sum_{i=1}^{n} p_i x_i$$

$$= \sum_{i=1}^{n} p'(x_i^2 - x_i) + \sum_{i=1}^{n} (p_i' - p_i) x_i$$

$$= \sum_{i=1}^{n} p_i'(x_i^2 - x_i) + x_j \Delta p_j$$

since only the jth price changes. Moreover if we allow Δp_j to become smaller and smaller, then the slopes of the two budget lines become closer and closer together until, in the limit, the movement from $(x_1 \ldots x_n)$ to $(x_1^2 \ldots x_n^2)$ is actually a movement along the tangent to the indifference curve at $\mathbf{x}$; that is a movement along the original budget line. This means that

$$\sum_{i=1}^{n} p_i'(x_i^2 - x_i) = 0$$

in the limit since both $\mathbf{x}$ and $\mathbf{x}^2$ lie on the same budget line. Hence in the limit $\mathrm{d}M = x_j \, \mathrm{d}p_j$. This then means that for infinitesimal price changes

$$\frac{\mathrm{d}x_i}{\mathrm{d}p_j}\bigg|_{\text{utility constant}} \mathrm{d}p_j = \left[\frac{\partial x_i}{\partial p_j} + x_j \frac{\partial x_i}{\partial M}\right] \mathrm{d}p_j$$

This equation is regarded as the keystone of traditional demand theory. It is known as the *Slutsky equation* and from it we can deduce the qualitative predictions of demand theory. Indeed we will, in the remainder of this section, largely be concerned with examining the nature of the offer curve in terms of this equation. Since this is so it is convenient to introduce the special notation for the left-hand side of the equation by writing

$$\frac{\mathrm{d}x_i}{\mathrm{d}p_j}\bigg|_{\text{utility constant}} \equiv \frac{\delta x_i}{\delta p_j}$$

which is known in the literature as the substitution effect. The term income effect refers to the expression $-x_j(\partial x_i/\partial M)$. Thus Slutsky's equation states that the total effect on x_i of a change in p_j can be expressed for every pair of goods as the sum of the income and substitution effects [56]:

$$\frac{\partial x_i}{\partial p_j} = \frac{\delta x_i}{\delta p_j} - x_j \frac{\partial x_i}{\lambda M}$$

These definitions of substitution effects correspond to those established in the literature [31]. Notice, however, that we could define many different sorts of substitution effects between a pair of goods i and j depending on which third variable we wish to change to compensate the consumer. For example, if there are three goods at least, i, j and k, we could define $\delta x_i/\delta p_j$ to be the change in purchases x_i due to a change in price of the jth good when the price of the kth good simultaneously changes to compensate the consumer. Thus as before

$$\frac{\delta x_i}{\delta p_j} dp_j = \frac{\partial x_i}{\partial p_j} dp_j + \frac{\partial x_i}{\partial p_k} \delta p_k$$

However, we can calculate δp_k along the same lines as before. To be able to just buy the original **x** after the simultaneous price changes (dp_j, δp_k) we must have

$$x_j \, dp_j + x_k \, \delta p_k = 0$$

Hence $\delta p_k = (-x_j/x_k) \, dp_j$ and so, following our previous argument

$$\frac{\delta x_i}{\delta p_j} dp_j = \left[\frac{\partial x_i}{\partial p_j} - \frac{x_j}{x_k} \frac{\partial x_i}{\partial p_k} \right] dp_j$$

We would then proceed to work out the properties of this type of substitution effect. The interested reader is referred to work in Houthakker [32]. Such a framework is particularly relevant to models of consumer choice in which consumer income is not exogenous but is chosen by the consumer; his income consisting of the hours he chooses to work valued at the exogenous ruling wage rate.

Much of the rest of traditional demand theory involves finding the properties of the income-compensated substitution effect. This being so we shall use a framework giving prominence to this substitution term [28, 43].

COST MINIMISATION

Suppose that we fix the level of utility and the vector of market prices and find the minimum expenditure which is necessary to reach the given level of utility. This minimum expenditure will obviously depend on prices and the level of utility, so that we have an expenditure or cost function

$$g(p_1 \ldots p_n, u) = \text{Min} \left\{ \sum_{i=1}^{n} p_i x_i \mid u(x_1 \ldots x_n) \geqslant u \right\}$$

where the notation $\text{Min}\{ . \mid . \}$ means that we minimise the first expression over all quantities satisfying the second expression.

Since the argument which follows is somewhat mathematical, we will attempt to present the essence of the argument by considering geometrically a two-dimensional illustration based on Shephard's work [55]. To use the expenditure or cost function approach we look at the consumer's problem from an alternative viewpoint. Instead of treating the slope and level of the budget line as fixed and finding the highest indifference curve attainable, we treat the slope of the budget line and the indifference curve we require to reach as fixed and then find the lowest income required to reach the fixed indifference curve. Geometrically we imagine moving the budget line of fixed slope out from the origin parallel to itself until it just allows the fixed indifference curve to be attained. Geometrically it is clear that either way of representing the consumer's problem yields the same answer. With the first approach we describe the solution to the problem by having utility as a function of the quantities which are utility maximising for a particular budgetary situation while with the second approach we have income or expenditure as a function of the quantities which are the cost minimising way of 'purchasing' a given utility level at fixed prices.

We wish to characterise the properties of the cost function $g(p_1, p_2, u)$ given that the individual has an indifference map represented by $u = u(x_1, x_2)$. At particular prices (p_1^*, p_2^*) and income we can find the highest indifference curve attainable

B

by the individual; this is labelled in the diagram as $u(x_1, x_2) = K$. This operation determines the optimising (x_1^*, x_2^*) to be purchased by the individual, shown in Fig. 10 by the line OX. The line perpendicular to the budget con-

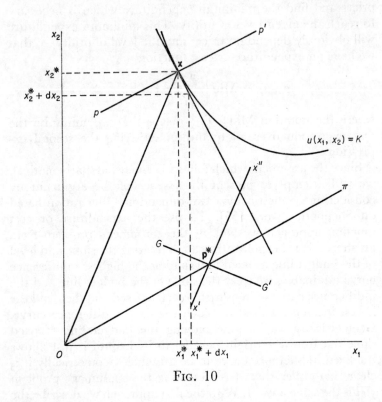

FIG. 10

straint, PP', must have a slope equal to p_1^*/p_2^* since this line has slope

$$\frac{\partial u(x_1^*, x_2^*)}{\partial x_1} \bigg/ \frac{\partial u(x_1^*, x_2^*)}{\partial x_2} = \frac{p_1^*}{p_2^*}$$

at (x_1^*, x_2^*), because at this point the budget line is tangential to the indifference curve. Now suppose that as well as measuring quantities on the axes, we also measure prices so that any pair of prices (p_1, p_2) can be represented by a point in the plane.

Then all points on the line $O\pi$, parallel to PP', represent pairs of prices (p_1, p_2) with the special property that the ratio of the first to the second price is equal to the price ratio p_1^*/p_2^*. Hence we can mark off along $O\pi$ the point $(p_1^*, p_2^*) = P^*$. We wish to plot the locus of all prices (p_1, p_2) which yield a fixed cheapest cost, M^*, of getting a utility level K. Then at (p_1^*, p_2^*) we can achieve K so that $g(p_1^*, p_2^*, K) = M^*$, and P^* is one point on this locus. We also know that $M^* = p_1^* x_1^* + p_2^* x_2^*$ and that if we make a small movement along the tangent to the indifference curve at $\mathbf{x}$, then $p_1^* \,\mathrm{d}x_1 + p_2^* \,\mathrm{d}x_2 = 0$ where $(\mathrm{d}x_1, \mathrm{d}x_2)$ is the small movement. Hence if we also make a small price change $(\mathrm{d}p_1, \mathrm{d}p_2)$ such that $x_1^* \,\mathrm{d}p_1 + x_2^* \,\mathrm{d}p_2 = 0$, then we know that cost and utility will both be constant. This tells us that at P^* the tangent to the constant cost locus must have a slope $\mathrm{d}p_1/\mathrm{d}p_2$ such that $x_1^* \,\mathrm{d}p_1 + x_2^* \,\mathrm{d}p_2 = 0$. But then if through P^*, we draw a line parallel to OX and labelled in the diagram as $X'X''$ then the required tangent to the constant cost locus at P^* must be perpendicular to the line $X'X''$ and hence must be represented by the line GG' in the diagram.

If we now vary the initial prices and income in such a way that the consumer can just maintain the level of utility K by purchasing different quantities of goods (x_1^{**}, x_2^{**}), then we have a new line $O\pi'$ with slope equal to the new price ratio p_1^{**}/p_2^{**} and we have to choose the point (p_1, p_2) on $O\pi'$ such that $p_1 x^{**} + p_2 x^{**} = M^*$ so that (p_1', p_2') lies on the same constant cost locus at P^*. Having found such a point (p_1', p_2') then the line through (p_1', p_2') with slope (x_1^{**}/x_2^{**}) must be the tangent to the constant cost locus at (p_1', p_2') for the same reasons as before. In this way we can generate all price combinations (p_1, p_2) which yield a constant cost of M^* attaining the given utility level K, together with the slope at each point (p_1, p_2) of the constant utility, constant cost locus. Under certain circumstances we can 'join up' each of these points to form a smooth constant cost locus whose slope at any point is given by

$$-\frac{\mathrm{d}p_1}{\mathrm{d}p_2} = \frac{x_2}{x_1}$$

But we know that the slope of the constant cost locus must also be capable of representation as

$$-\frac{\mathrm{d}p_1}{\mathrm{d}p_2} = \frac{\partial g(p_1, p_2, K)}{\partial p_2} \Big/ \frac{\partial g(p_1, p_2, K)}{\partial p_1}$$

since if cost and utility are constant we must have

$$\mathrm{d}g = \frac{\partial g(p_1, p_2, K)}{\partial p_1}\,\mathrm{d}p_1 + \frac{\partial g(p_1, p_2, K)}{\partial p_2}\,\mathrm{d}p_2 = 0$$

Hence we have the result that for utility constant,

$$\frac{\partial g(p_1, p_2, K)}{\partial p_i} = x_i$$

where the x_i are the cost minimising quantities.

We can also easily demonstrate that the constant cost loci for different cost levels look exactly the same as one another in

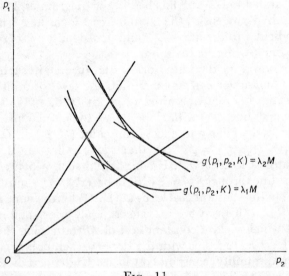

FIG. 11

the sense that if we keep p_1/p_2 constant and vary the cost level then the slope of the cost contour at any given level of cost must be the same as at any other given level of cost (Fig. 11). This is because if (x_1^*, x_2^*) is the cheapest way of attaining utility level K at (p_1^*, p_2^*) at a cost of M^*, then (x_1^*, x_2^*) is also the cheapest way of attaining utility level K at prices $(\lambda p_1^*, \lambda p_2^*)$ and at a cost of $\lambda M^* = \lambda p_1^* x_1^* + \lambda p_2^* x_2^*$. But the slope of the constant cost locus is given by the quantities (x_1^*, x_2^*) under proportional variations in prices $(\lambda p_1^*, \lambda p_2^*)$ and costs which keep price ratios constant. Hence slopes of the different constant cost contours at given relative prices are equal.

Mathematically this is expressed by saying that the cost function $g(p_1, p_2, u)$ is homogeneous of degree one in prices.

Summarising the argument, we have deduced various properties of the cost function in the two-dimensional case. In fact these properties do not depend on the restriction that there be only two goods. In general with n goods at the cost minimising point

$$g(p_1 \ldots p_n, K) = \sum_{i=1}^{n} p_i x_i^*$$

where the x_i^* are demands at prices $(p_1 \ldots p_n)$ and income $g(p_1 \ldots p_n, K)$. Moreover in general

$$x_i = \frac{\partial g(p_1 \ldots p_n, K)}{\partial p_i}$$

so that we have expressed quantities demanded in terms of prices and the utility through partial derivatives of $g(\mathbf{p}, u)$. These demand functions are often referred to as *compensated demand functions* since if we vary p_j, keeping all other prices and utility constant, then quantities change according to

$$\frac{\delta x_i}{\delta p_j} = \frac{\partial^2 g(\mathbf{p}, u)}{\partial p_j \, \partial p_i}$$

Hence second order partial derivatives of $g(\mathbf{p}, u)$ are just the substitution effects already discussed. We have also found that if prices double then cost minimising quantities are unchanged but cost doubles. Finally, the constant cost loci for fixed utility are downward sloping curves convex to the origin.

As a useful exercise the reader is invited to work out the shape of the constant cost contours in the case in which each indifference curve consists of a right-angled curve, with the 'sides' of the angle being vertically upwards and horizontally to the right of the angle.

To deduce the behaviour of the substitution effect we have to express some of the above properties of the last function in slightly more mathematical language. The expenditure function $g(\mathbf{p}, u)$ is concave in prices: i.e. its contours are convex to the origin in price space. Mathematically a function $f(x_1 \ldots x_n)$ is concave if for any two points $(x_1^0 \ldots x_n^0)$ $(x_1' \ldots x_n')$ at which it is defined and for any number λ between 0 and 1

$$f\{\lambda \mathbf{x}^0 + (1 - \lambda)\ \mathbf{x}'\} \geqslant \lambda f(\mathbf{x}^0) + (1 - \lambda) f(\mathbf{x}')$$

To check that g is concave in prices hold the level of utility constant at U and let $(p_1^1 \ldots p_n^1)$ and $(p_1^2 \ldots p_n^2)$ be any two price collections. Also let $\mathbf{x}^1$ and $\mathbf{x}^2$ be the cost-minimising bundles at the prices $\mathbf{p}^1$ and $\mathbf{p}^2$ respectively. Then

$$\sum p_i^1 x_i^1 = g(\mathbf{p}^1, u)$$
$$\sum p_i^2 x_i^2 = g(\mathbf{p}^2, u)$$

Let $\bar{\mathbf{x}} = (\bar{x}_1 \ldots \bar{x}_n)$ be cost minimising at some weighted average of the prices $\lambda \mathbf{p}^1 + (1 - \lambda)\ \mathbf{p}^2$. But $\mathbf{x}^1$, $\mathbf{x}^2$, $\bar{\mathbf{x}}$ all satisfy the same constraint; namely they each yield utility levels of at least U. Hence

$$\sum p_i^1 x_i^1 = g(\mathbf{p}^1, u) \leqslant \sum p_i^1 \bar{x}_i$$
$$\sum p_i^2 x_i^2 = g(\mathbf{p}^2, u) \leqslant \sum p_i^2 \bar{x}_i$$

Multiplying the first inequality by $\lambda \geqslant 0$ and the second by $(1 - \lambda) \geqslant 0$ and adding yields the following

$$\lambda g(\mathbf{p}^1, u) + (1 - \lambda)\ g(\mathbf{p}^2, u) \leqslant \sum_{i=1}^{n} |\ \lambda p_i^1 + (1 - \lambda)\ p_i^2\ |\ \bar{x}_i$$
$$= g(\lambda \mathbf{p}^1 + (1 - \lambda)\ \mathbf{p}^2, u)$$

The economic intuition of this result lies in the fact that for every pair of goods there is a diminishing marginal rate of substitution, i.e. the indifference curves are convex to the origin. If we make one good successively cheaper relative to the other goods, then the minimum expenditure required to reach a given indifference curve will involve substituting the cheaper good for other goods. Hence the minimum expenditure will fall; but due to the diminishing marginal rate of substitution, the possibilities of substitution are limited and so the minimum expenditure will fall at a decreasing rate. As increasing amounts of the good which has become relatively cheap are purchased the marginal rate of substitution between that good and other goods falls, implying that increasing quantities of the cheaper good must be purchased to substitute for one unit of any other good and to keep utility constant.

But for any concave function it happens to be true that

$$\frac{\partial^2 g(\mathbf{p}, u)}{\partial p_i^2} \leqslant 0$$

and

$$\sum_{i=1}^{n} \sum_{j=1}^{n} \frac{\partial^2 g(\mathbf{p}, u)}{\partial p_i \, p_j} \, \mathrm{d}p_i \, \mathrm{d}p_j \leqslant 0$$

for any changes $\mathrm{d}p_i \, \mathrm{d}p_j$ [36]. These inequalities will prove extremely useful.

Secondly, for any sufficiently smooth function $g(\mathbf{p}, u)$, we have

$$\frac{\partial^2 g(\mathbf{p}, u)}{\partial p_i \, \partial p_j} = \frac{\partial^2 g(\mathbf{p}, u)}{\partial p_j \, \partial p_i}$$

Now using the expression for the substitution effect in terms of $g(\mathbf{p}, u)$, it is true that

$$\frac{\delta x_i}{\delta p_j} = \frac{\delta x_j}{\delta p_i} \quad (\text{for all } i \text{ and } j)$$

From our earlier inequalities we also know that

$$\frac{\delta x_i}{\delta p_i} \leqslant 0 \quad (i = 1 \ldots n) \qquad \sum_{i=1}^{n} \sum_{j=1}^{n} \frac{\delta x_i}{\delta p_j} \, \mathrm{d}p_i \, \mathrm{d}p_j \leqslant 0$$

while by the homogeneity of $g(p, u)$ Euler's law holds:

$$\sum_{i=1}^{n} p_i \frac{\partial g(p, u)}{\partial p_i} = g(\mathbf{p}, u)$$

and so, on differentiating this with respect to p_j, we have

$$\sum_{i=1}^{n} p_i \frac{\delta x_i}{\delta p_j} + x_j = x_j$$

leading to $\displaystyle\sum_{i=1}^{n} p_i \frac{\delta x_i}{\delta p_j} = 0$. These properties contain the prediction

of demand theory. Since

$$\frac{\partial x_i}{\partial p_i} = -x_i \frac{\partial x_i}{\partial M} + \frac{\delta x_i}{\delta p_i}$$

we know that so long as $\partial x_i / \partial M$ is always positive an increase in the price of a good will lead to a fall in the equilibrium purchases of the good. If, however, $\partial x_i / \partial M < 0$ and is sufficiently strong to outweigh the substitution effect then we have the well-known *Giffen case* in which an increased price is associated with increased consumption of the good. Various other deductions are possible: if there are only two goods (x_1, x_2) then the fact that

$$\frac{\delta x_1}{\delta p_1} \leqslant 0 \quad \text{and that} \quad p_1 \frac{\delta x_1}{\delta p_1} + p_2 \frac{\delta x_1}{\delta p_2} = 0$$

means that we must have $(\delta x_1 / \delta p_2) \geqslant 0$ for all non-negative prices: as will be seen later, goods standing in this relationship are referred to as *substitutes*.

We can also infer from our inequalities that the sum of expenditure changes on all goods due to a given proportional change in each price must be non-positive. Thus

$$\sum_{i=1}^{n} \sum_{j=1}^{n} \frac{\delta x_i}{\delta p_j} \, \mathrm{d}p_i \, \mathrm{d}p_j \leqslant 0 \text{ must hold for all values of } \mathrm{d}p_i \text{ and so}$$

if we set $\mathrm{d}p_i = p_i$ the equation certainly holds. But then

$$\sum_{i=1}^{n} \sum_{i=1}^{n} \frac{\partial x_i}{\partial p_j} p_i p_j = \sum_{j=1}^{n} -x_j p_j \sum_{i=1}^{n} p_i \frac{\partial x_i}{\partial M} + \sum_{j=1}^{n} p_j \sum_{i=1}^{n} p_i \frac{\delta x_i}{\delta p_j}$$

$$\leqslant -\sum_{j=1}^{n} x_j p_j \quad \text{since} \quad \sum p_i \frac{\partial x_i}{\partial M} = 1$$

as all income is spent.

Hence $$\sum_{i=1}^{n} \sum_{j=1}^{n} \frac{\partial x_i}{\partial p_j} p_i p_j \leqslant 0$$

But this can be rewritten

$$\sum_{i=1}^{n} \sum_{j=1}^{n} \frac{\partial(p_i x_i)}{(\partial p_j / p_j)} < 0$$

which gives us the above statement.

SOME 'PATHOLOGICAL' CASES

After the previous rather general arguments, it is useful to consider some less abstract examples. Suppose a consumer does not everywhere satisfy the convexity axiom but has indifference curves like those in Fig. 12. Then, so long as there are positive prices for each good and the consumer is maximising, he will never purchase a bundle like $\mathbf{x}^*$ since there will always be a

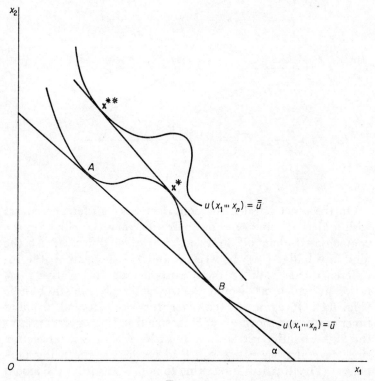

FIG. 12

bundle like $\mathbf{x}^{**}$ in the convex part of an indifference curve which could be purchased and which would yield a higher utility level. If we plot the compensated demand functions giving x_i/x_j as a function of relative prices as we move around any one indifference curve, then at the price ratio a any ratio of quantities between that corresponding to point A and that to point B may be purchased. Hence the compensated demand functions will have a vertical section at some relative price (Fig. 13).

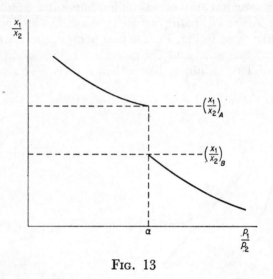

FIG. 13

On the other hand if the consumer has indifference curves with a kink at some ratio of quantities, then the effect on the compensated demand functions is rather different. At the kink any budget line between a and β is tangent to the indifference curve and so there exists a range of relative price ratios at which $\mathbf{x}^*$ would be the optimally chosen bundle (Fig. 14). If again we consider the compensated demand functions as we move around the fixed indifference curve, at the kink quantity ratios these must have a horizontal section since several price ratios will lead to this bundle being purchased (Fig. 15). It is interesting to note that within the axiom system for preferences, it is perfectly possible for the indifference curves to possess kinks, and yet such a case yields results which are not very convenient for economic analysis and are typically ignored. A more fundamental example of the violation of our system is that in which the consumer, perhaps because he is the sole buyer of a pair of goods, possesses some power over the prices at which he purchases so that the budget constraint

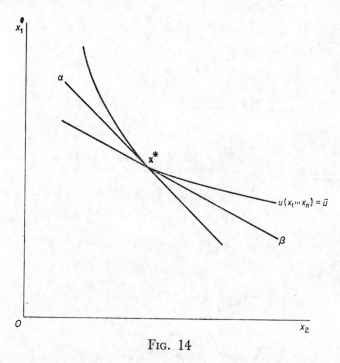

FIG. 14

is no longer a fixed straight line. Thus suppose that the price ratio p_i/p_j which the consumer faces depends on the ratio of the quantities x_i/x_j which he buys in such a way that as the consumer increases his ratio x_i/x_j then the price ratio p_i/p_j falls. Then if the price-ratio changes occur in a smooth way, a possible budget constraint for the consumer is that shown in Fig. 16. As we move from left to right round the curve the ratio x_i/x_j increases and the slope of the curve (p_i/p_j) falls. This is the case where bulk purchases by a consumer give him an increased power over his suppliers. The consumer can then

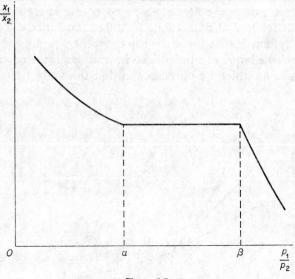

FIG. 15

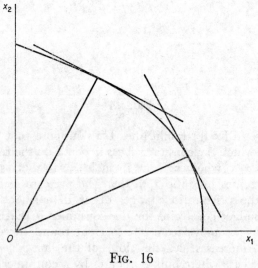

FIG. 16

proceed to maximise his utility level subject to his budget constraint and generally achieve a well-defined and unique maximising bundle and price ratio, so that we may apply the standard theory (Fig. 17). However, if the consumer's power over prices is in the reverse direction, which might be the case where suppliers fiercely compete for the marginal consumer of

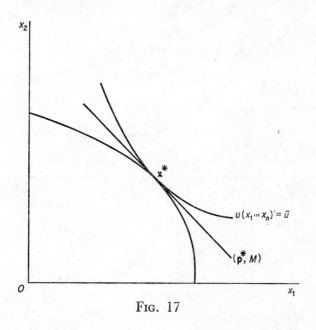

$$u(x_1 \cdots x_n) = \bar{u}$$

$$(\overset{*}{p}, M)$$

FIG. 17

their products, there are many possibilities demonstrated in Figs. 18–20 and the maximum certainly may not be unique. Mention might also be made of indifference curves displaying satiation either with respect to one good or with respect to all goods. If the consumer has a region in which he is satiated with respect to purchases of one good, then in this region, his indifference must pass through a point at which it has either horizontal or vertical slope and move on to bend backwards. Thus, bundle A in Fig. 21 will only be chosen if the budget line has a vertical slope and hence if the price of the jth good is zero while bundles along AB will only be chosen at a negative price for good j. Similar results hold along the section CD.

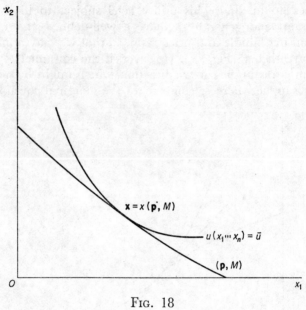

FIG. 18

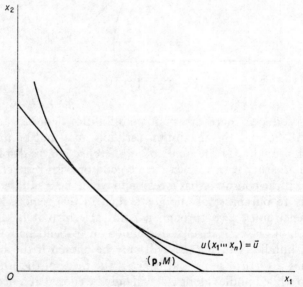

FIG. 19

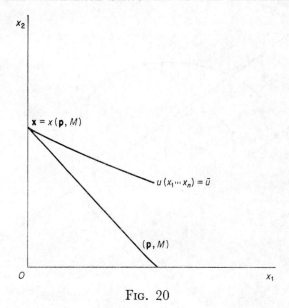

FIG. 20

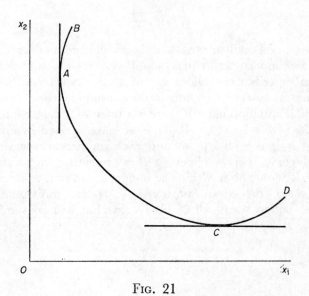

FIG. 21

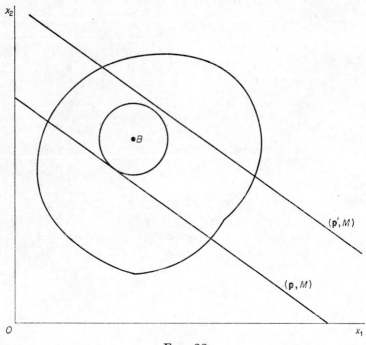

FIG. 22

This situation really means that, if we insist free goods can never be of any importance in an economic system (since an economic system describes the allocation of *scarce* resources), then we can never observe the individual consuming these bundles. A similar situation holds if there is a point of absolute satiation or bliss with respect to all goods as demonstrated in Fig. 22, where B is the bliss point and each indifference curve is a closed curve, curves closer to B representing higher utility levels. Then if B lies within the budget constraint, as would be the case if the constraint was (p', M), the individual will choose not to spend all of his income but will consume the bundle B.

3 Revealed Preference and Integrability

Market behaviour, i.e. the commodity bundles that individuals choose in different price/income situations, is in principle directly observable provided we can observe an infinite variety of price and income situations. On the other hand we cannot directly observe the tastes of individuals other than by asking them explicitly to state their preference orderings between commodity bundles or by constructing a laboratory experiment in which individuals are offered alternative bundles. However, many individuals may not determine their behaviour by reference to their implicit preference ordering, and individuals will generally have only a rather vague notion of their preferences. Can we then use the observed market behaviour of individuals to deduce a 'behaviour function' which individuals, through their acts, try to maximise? Can predictions as to the effects of changes in the price/income situation be made solely on the basis of observed market behaviour? If observed market behaviour satisfies particular conditions, then both of these problems can be resolved. The first problem largely falls into the domain of *integrability*, while the second lies within the realm of *revealed preference analysis*. It would appear that we can deduce a theory of demand without explicit reference to indifference curves at all, and hence derive a theory expressed only in terms of observable variables. However, since our qualitative conclusions will coincide with those that we would have deduced from the preference ordering framework one would expect that the conditions relating to the market observations must be of similar force to those on the preference ordering.

THE AXIOM SYSTEM

Samuelson [52] has developed a rather elegant framework for deducing the results of traditional demand theory through a system of axioms restricting the possible collections of observed choices in different market situations. The first two axioms have an immediate meaning and deal with defining the domain of discourse to be covered by the theory.

Axiom 1. In any price income situation $(\mathbf{p}, M)$, where all prices and income are positive, the consumer chooses a bundle $\mathbf{x}^0$ such that $\sum_{i=1}^{n} p_i x_i^0 = M$

Axiom 2. Every bundle $\mathbf{x}$ which is non-negative is chosen in some price/income situation.

The first axiom serves to define the class of price and income situations to be included and also ensures both that choice is definite in any situation and that in all situations there is never satiation; however low the prices or high the income there will always be a bundle chosen which just exhausts the available income. Despite the breadth of the price/income situations covered, and hence the restrictiveness of the theory in that choice must be well defined for extreme situations, the axiom is in fact unexceptionable. Evidently some such axiom is necessary and a much more restricted collection of market situations could be covered and would allow us to deduce the results for the more restricted domain. The second axiom essentially states that everything has its price. However, since we require positive prices, this may be restrictive: for example, an avowed ascetic might not choose to purchase a bundle containing very large quantities of, say, caviar at any non-negative price situation. The force of this axiom is really to rule out the possibility of satiation with respect to a single good: i.e. the consumer must find all goods desirable.

To state the third axiom we must introduce some new concepts: let any particular price income situation $(\mathbf{p}^0, M^0)$ prevail and let $\mathbf{x}^0$ be the bundle chosen in this situation. Let $\mathbf{x}$ be any bundle such that $\sum_{i=1}^{n} p_i^0 x_i \leqslant M^0$ so that in the situation

($\mathbf{p}^0$, M^0) the consumer could, if he had wished, have afforded to purchase $\mathbf{x}$. However, since the consumer actually chose $\mathbf{x}^0$ rather than $\mathbf{x}$ although both were available to him, his behaviour has 'revealed' $\mathbf{x}^0$ to be preferred to $\mathbf{x}$. This is a useful definition of '$\mathbf{x}^0$ being revealed preferred to $\mathbf{x}$' and can be formalised by the notation $\mathbf{x} \ominus \mathbf{x}^0$, signifying precisely that $\mathbf{x}$ is revealed inferior to $\mathbf{x}^0$. In other words for any two bundles $\mathbf{x}$, $\mathbf{x}^0$

$$\mathbf{x} \ominus \mathbf{x}^0 \quad \text{if and only if} \quad \sum_{i=1}^{n} p_i^0 x_i \leqslant \sum_{i=1}^{n} p_i^0 x_i^0$$

Logical consistency requires that if there is a bundle $\mathbf{x}^0$ which is not revealed preferred to some bundle $\mathbf{x}$, then it cannot be true that

$$\sum_{i=1}^{n} p_i^0 x_i \leqslant \sum_{i=1}^{n} p_i^0 x_i^0$$

and hence it must be true that

$$\sum_{i=1}^{n} p_i^0 x_i > \sum_{i=1}^{n} p_i^0 x_i^0$$

Formally a property of the relation $\ominus$ is that {not $\mathbf{x} \ominus \mathbf{x}^0$} means; we have $\Sigma p_i^0 x_i > p_i^0 x_i^0$. It should also be noted that for any $\mathbf{x}^0$ we have $\mathbf{x}^0 \ominus \mathbf{x}^0$. Our third axiom on consumer behaviour then states that if $\mathbf{x}^0$ is revealed preferred to $\mathbf{x}^1$ (where $\mathbf{x}^0 \neq \mathbf{x}^1$) then $\mathbf{x}^1$ cannot simultaneously be revealed[1] preferred to $\mathbf{x}^0$.

Axiom 3. $\mathbf{x}^1 \ominus \mathbf{x}^0$ and $\mathbf{x}^0 \neq \mathbf{x}^1$ mean that we cannot have $\mathbf{x}^0 \ominus \mathbf{x}^1$.

Appealing to the definition of $\ominus$ the axiom can be stated alternatively as: whenever $\Sigma p_i^0 x_i^0 \geqslant \Sigma p_i^0 x_i^1$ then it must be true that $\Sigma p_i^1 x_i^1 < \Sigma p_i^1 x_i^0$. In words, if at the prices and income at which $\mathbf{x}^0$ is chosen, the consumer has sufficient income to purchase the bundle $\mathbf{x}^1$ then at the prices and income at which $\mathbf{x}^1$ is the chosen bundle, the consumer must not have sufficient income to purchase $\mathbf{x}^0$. This is evidently a consistency condition on tastes: if, of two available alternatives $\mathbf{x}^0$, $\mathbf{x}^1$, the consumer chooses $\mathbf{x}^0$ then when the consumer actually chooses $\mathbf{x}^1$ in a different situation, $\mathbf{x}^0$ must not be available. Stated in this way, the condition appears to be nothing more than a requirement that consumer behaviour should be consistent between alternative situations. In fact the axiom states more than this: in the $(\mathbf{p}^1, M^1)$ situation, $\mathbf{x}^0$ is not available because it is too expensive: from this last clause we can see that the condition leads to convexity of choices. Thus suppose we find the loci of all commodity bundles which are not revealed preferred to one another. Then axiom 3,

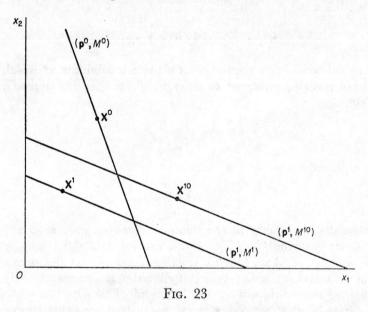

Fig. 23

known in the literature as the *weak axiom of revealed preference*, provides a basis for proving that these loci must be strictly convex to the origin. Figure 23 illustrates the type of argument. Let $\mathbf{x}^0$ chosen at $(\mathbf{p}^0, M^0)$ be revealed preferred to $\mathbf{x}^1$. Then by axiom 3 we must have

$$\sum_{i=1}^{n} p_i^1 x_i^0 > \sum_{i=1}^{n} p_i^1 x_i^1$$

This will certainly be the case if the budget line corresponding to $(\mathbf{p}^1, M^1)$ has a flatter slope than that corresponding to $(\mathbf{p}^0, M^0)$. But then since $\mathbf{x}^0$ is revealed preferred to $\mathbf{x}^1$ then, if it is possible to find a bundle $\mathbf{x}^{10}$, such that neither $\mathbf{x}^{10}$ nor

$\mathbf{x}^0$ are revealed preferred to one another and such that $\mathbf{x}^{10}$ is chosen at $\mathbf{p}^1$ but with a higher income than M^1, then $\mathbf{x}^{10}$ must lie to the north-east of $\mathbf{x}^1$. But then $\mathbf{x}$ and $\mathbf{x}^0$ lie on the same locus and diagrammatically it is obvious that this locus must be convex to the origin. Hence in this sense the weak axiom of revealed preference is a convexity condition.

METHODS OF REVEALED PREFERENCE ANALYSIS

We can use this system of axioms to deduce many of the conclusions of traditional demand theory [52, 53, 45]. Thus it is easy to see that while the first axiom guarantees that some bundle will be chosen in any $(\mathbf{p}, M)$ situation the third axiom ensures that there will be only one bundle chosen in each situation. If at any given $(\mathbf{p}, M)$ there were two distinct bundles $\mathbf{x}^*$, $\mathbf{x}^{**}$ both chosen, then since $\Sigma p_i x_i^* = \Sigma p_i x_i^{**}$ by non-satiation, we have both $\mathbf{x}^* \otimes \mathbf{x}^{**}$ and $\mathbf{x}^{**} \otimes \mathbf{x}^*$ which is impossible if the third axiom holds. Thus we can deduce that a well-defined system of demand functions $x_i = f^i(\mathbf{p}, M)$ exists for each $(\mathbf{p}, M)$. The intuition of this statement is that the third axiom ensures the 'revealed indifferent' loci referred to above have a form strictly convex to the origin and hence for any positive prices, there will exist a unique point at which the budget line defined by these prices is tangential to the revealed indifferent locus.

We can also show that if all prices and income are multiplied up by any proportionality factor λ, then the bundle chosen in the two situations is unchanged. Thus let $\mathbf{x}^0$ be chosen at $(\mathbf{p}^0, M^0)$ and let $\mathbf{x}^{00}$ be chosen at $(\lambda p_1^0 \dots \lambda p_n^0; \lambda M^0)$. We have $\Sigma p_i^0 x_i^0 = M^0$ and $\Sigma \lambda p_i^0 x_i^{00} = \lambda \Sigma p_i^0 x_i^{00} = \lambda M^0$ by the first axiom. But then we have $\mathbf{x}^{00} \otimes \mathbf{x}^0$ since $\mathbf{x}^{00}$ could be purchased at $(\mathbf{p}^0, M^0)$ and so by the third axiom we must have that if $\mathbf{x}^{00} \neq \mathbf{x}^0$ then $\lambda \Sigma p_i^0 x_i^0 > \lambda \Sigma p_i^0 x_i^0 > \lambda \Sigma p_i^0 x_i^{00}$. But $\lambda \Sigma p_i^0 x_i^0 = \lambda M^0$ and hence $\mathbf{x}^{00}$ does not use up all of the income in the situation $(\lambda p_1^0 \dots \lambda p_n^0; \lambda M^0)$ in which it is chosen. This is impossible if the first axiom holds and hence it must be true that $\mathbf{x}^0 = \mathbf{x}^{00}$: the chosen bundle is in fact the same in the two situations.

We can also deduce [43] that a form of the generalised substitution effect is non-positive. Thus let

$$x_i^0 = f^i(\mathbf{p}^0, M^0) \qquad x_i^1 = f^i(\mathbf{p}^1, M^1)$$

and let $x_i^{10} = f^i(\mathbf{p}_i, \Sigma p_i^1 x_i^0)$ so that $\mathbf{x}^{10}$ is the bundle chosen at the new prices $\mathbf{p}^1$ when the consumer has just sufficient income

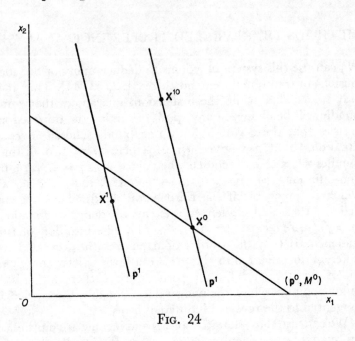

FIG. 24

to purchase $\mathbf{x}^0$ at these prices as in Fig. 24. We wish to show that if prices change from $\mathbf{p}^0$ to $\mathbf{p}^1$ and income also changes to allow the consumer just to purchase his original choice then the sum of the products of price changes with quantity changes is non-positive, i.e. $\underset{i}{\Sigma}(p_i^1 - p_i^0)(x_i^{10} - x_i^0) \leqslant 0$ and that strict inequality holds whenever $\mathbf{x}^0 \neq \mathbf{x}^{10}$. It is sufficient to show that $\Sigma p_i^1(x_i^{10} - x_i^0) \leqslant 0$ if $\mathbf{x}^0 \neq \mathbf{x}^{10}$ and $\Sigma p_i^0(x_i^{10} - x_i^0) \geqslant 0$ if $\mathbf{x}^0 \neq \mathbf{x}^{10}$, with at least one of these inequalities having a strict form. However, it is obvious that since the consumer always spends the whole of his income it must be true that $\Sigma p_i^1 x_i^{10} = \Sigma p_i^1 x_i^0$, since the left-hand side is his expenditure following the price and income change, while the right-hand side is his income. But, by the third axiom, since $\mathbf{x}^{10}$ is chosen when $\mathbf{x}^0$ was available it must be true that $\mathbf{x}^{10}$ is not available when $\mathbf{x}^0$ is chosen: i.e. we must have $\Sigma p_i^0 x_i^{10} > \Sigma p_i^0 x_i^0$ so long as $\mathbf{x}^0 \neq \mathbf{x}^{10}$. Hence as long as $\mathbf{x}^{10} \neq \mathbf{x}^0$ then $\Sigma(p_i^1 - p_i^0)$ $(x_i^{10} - x_i^0) < 0$ while if $\mathbf{x}^{10} = \mathbf{x}^0$, so that the same bundle is chosen in the two price income situations, then

$$\Sigma(p_i^1 - p_i^0)(x_i^{10} - x_i^0) = 0.$$

Note that this proof is independent of the relationship between $\mathbf{x}^0$ and $\mathbf{x}^1$: we may have either $\mathbf{x}^0 \oslash \mathbf{x}^1$ or $\mathbf{x}^1 \oslash \mathbf{x}^0$ as Fig. 25 shows.

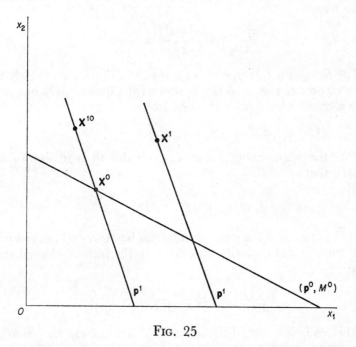

FIG. 25

Note also that if we consider price changes in only a single good, say the ith good, together with the corresponding income change, then since every term in $(\mathbf{p}^1 - \mathbf{p}^0)$ except the ith is zero we have $(p_i^1 - p_i^0)(x_i^{10} - x_i^0) < 0$ so long as $\mathbf{x}^{10} \neq \mathbf{x}^0$, so that if the price of any single good rises and income changes to compensate, then purchases of the good fall. This is the analogous result in revealed preference theory to the fact that the own substitution effect $\delta x_i / \delta p_i$ is negative, although since we are defining the compensating change in income in a rather different fashion we should be wary of identifying the change from $\mathbf{x}^0$ to $\mathbf{x}^{10}$ immediately as the traditional substitution effect.

We can in fact [52 61] split up the movement from $\mathbf{x}^0$ to $\mathbf{x}^1$ as prices change from $\mathbf{p}^0$ to $\mathbf{p}^1$ with income constant, into movements analogous to substitution and income effects. Suppose as before that only the ith price changes so that we may write $\mathbf{p}^1 = (p_1^0 \ldots p_i^0 + \Delta p_i \ldots p_n^0)$. Then, for any good j, we have

$$\frac{x_j^1 - x_j^0}{\Delta p_i} = \frac{x_j^1 - x_j^{10}}{\Delta p_i} + \frac{x_j^{10} - x_j^0}{\Delta p_i}$$

The first term corresponds to a quantity change due solely to an income change and the second term a quantity change due to a compensated price change. Indeed we have

$$\Delta M = \sum p_i^0 x_i^0 - \sum p_i^1 x_i^0 = -x_i^0 \, \Delta p_i$$

since the price change occurs only for the ith good. Hence we have that

$$\frac{1}{\Delta p_i} = -\frac{x_i^0}{\Delta M}$$

or the inverse of the price change can be expressed as the ratio of the original quantity purchased to the income change and so

$$\frac{x_j^1 - x_j^0}{\Delta p_i} = -x_i^0 \frac{(x_j^1 - x_j^{10})}{\Delta M} + \frac{(x_j^{10} - x_j^0)}{\Delta p_i}$$

This equation already bears a close relation to the Slutsky equation and it is true that as the price change becomes infinitesimally small then under certain technical conditions, this equation reduces to

$$\frac{\partial x_j}{\partial p_i} = -x_i \frac{\partial x_j}{\partial m} + \frac{\delta x_j}{\delta p_i}$$

where the last term measures the change in x_j coming from a simultaneous change in p_i and in income. However, instead of changing income to remain on the same indifference curve we have changed income to allow the original bundle still to be purchased in the new price situation. As the price change becomes very small it can be shown that these two income changes coincide, and we can interpret the last term as the Hicks substitution effect. For any finite price change, however, the two will differ and for this reason Samuelson has referred to the last term as the 'overcompensated' substitution effect, since, typically, if indifference curves existed then the income change would allow the consumer to move to a higher indifference curve than in the original situation. We have, therefore, from our axiom system been able to deduce the basic theorems of traditional demand analysis without explicitly ever referring to indifference curves. Since we have the same conclusions, it is natural to enquire whether our axiom system allows us to deduce the existence of curves having all the usual properties of indifference curves such that the consumer's behaviour can be treated as the result of using these curves as if they were true indifference curves. In other words, can we show from our axiom system that there must exist a function which we can interpret as a utility function? If this were possible, then market behaviour would have to allow us to define an ordering of commodity bundles satisfying all the conditions of the preference ordering of Chapter 1 so that this 'preference' ordering could actually be represented by a utility function. In order for this to be possible we require, amongst other things, that the ordering be transitive and also that it satisfies technical smoothness conditions. However, if we start from our three revealed preference axioms, any derived ordering must be based on these, and in particular on the notion of 'being revealed preferred to'. Our third axiom and the relation of revealed preference deal only with *pairs* of commodity bundles and say nothing about the relation between triples of bundles. We cannot necessarily deduce from $\mathbf{x} \oslash \mathbf{y}$ and $\mathbf{y} \oslash \mathbf{z}$ that $\mathbf{x} \oslash \mathbf{z}$.

Hence without some additional restrictions we cannot expect to deduce transitivity of any ordering based on revealed preference. The situation is summarised in Fig. 26: suppose we have $\mathbf{y} \oslash \mathbf{x}$, $\mathbf{z} \oslash \mathbf{y}$ and $\mathbf{x} \oslash \mathbf{z}$ and let us find all bundles revealed inferior to each of $\mathbf{x}$, $\mathbf{y}$, $\mathbf{z}$ respectively, and represent these bundles by the areas under curves along which bundles are not revealed inferior to one another. If we then try to

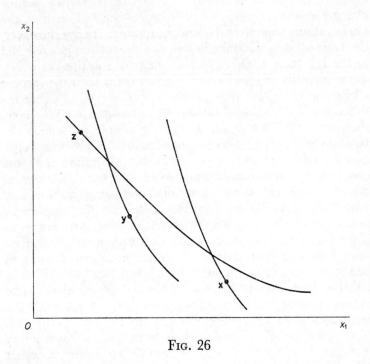

Fig. 26

interpret these curves as indifference curves we see that due to the lack of transitivity in the implicit ordering they intersect.

We can introduce a transitivity condition to our axiom system in the following way. First let us define the notion of 'being indirectly revealed preferred to' as holding between two bundles $\mathbf{x}$, $\mathbf{y}$ if we can find some finite chain of bundles $(\mathbf{u}_1, \mathbf{u}_2 \ldots \mathbf{u}_m)$ such that each pair of bundles $(\mathbf{u}_i, \mathbf{u}_{i+1})$ stand in the direct revealed preference relation to one another and also $(\mathbf{x}, \mathbf{u}_1)$ and $(\mathbf{u}_m, \mathbf{y})$ stand in the direct revealed preference relation. Formally write $\mathbf{x} Q \mathbf{y}$ to indicate that $\mathbf{y}$ is indirectly revealed preferred to $\mathbf{x}$. Then $\mathbf{x}Q\mathbf{y}$ if and only if there exists a chain $(\mathbf{u}_1 \ldots \mathbf{u}_m)$ of finite length m such that

$$\mathbf{x} \otimes \mathbf{u}_1 \otimes \mathbf{u}_2 \otimes \ldots \otimes \mathbf{u}_m \otimes \mathbf{y}.$$

Our transitivity condition is designed to rule out the possibility of indirect 'loops' in the revealed preference relation, i.e. we want to rule out the possibility that for some $(\mathbf{u}_1 \ldots \mathbf{u}_m)$ and some $(\mathbf{w}_1 \ldots \mathbf{w}_p)$ we have

$$\mathbf{x} \otimes \mathbf{u}_1 \otimes \ldots \otimes \mathbf{u}_m \otimes \mathbf{y} \otimes \mathbf{w}_1 \otimes \ldots \otimes \mathbf{w}_p \otimes \mathbf{x}$$

and we can do this by requiring as a postulate:

Axiom 4: If $\mathbf{x}Q\mathbf{y}$ is true, then $\mathbf{y}Q\mathbf{x}$ is not true for any pair of bundles $\mathbf{x}$, $\mathbf{y}$. This condition, first introduced in [32], is known as the *strong axiom of revealed preference*. Since if axiom 4 holds axiom 3 obviously holds, we can replace axiom 3 by axiom 4 and use the modified axiom system as the basis for argument. It is also clear that if axiom 4 holds it is impossible to have a situation in which we have $\mathbf{y} \otimes \mathbf{x} \otimes \mathbf{z}$ and $\mathbf{z} \otimes \mathbf{y}$ as in Fig. 26, or any more indirect intransitivity. It is therefore not surprising that if we take each bundle $\mathbf{x}$ and find all other bundles which are neither indirectly revealed preferred nor inferior to $\mathbf{x}$ then, for two distinct bundles $\mathbf{x}$, $\mathbf{y}$ these loci of 'revealed indifferent' bundles will either coincide or never intersect. On the basis of non-satiation we can deduce that these loci must be downward-sloping curves, since if they contained 'thick' bands, as in Fig. 27, then there would be two bundles $\mathbf{x}$, $\mathbf{y}$ within the band such that $\mathbf{x}$ would be revealed preferred to $\mathbf{y}$. From the fact that the strong axiom implies the weak axiom and that if the weak axiom holds then choices are convex we can deduce that the curves are strictly convex to the origin. Furthermore each bundle on the curve is by construction chosen at the price ratio and income represented by the tangent to the curve. Hence our family of 'revealed indifferent' curves have all the properties of indifference curves deduced from a preference ordering. Hence, if consumer behaviour follows the first two postulates and the strong axiom of revealed preference, we can treat the consumer as if he were endowed with a utility function which he tries to maximise. Hence this axiom system and that of Chapter 1, although one

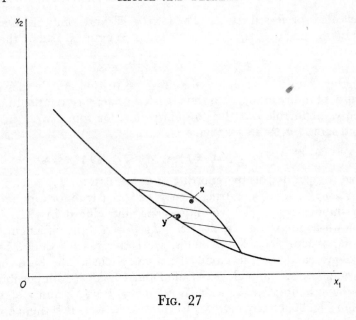

FIG. 27

starts with commodity bundles and the other with price and income situations, are formally equivalent.

We can, however, weaken our axiom system and still deduce the results of demand theory and the existence of a utility function as Richter [51] has demonstrated. In particular we can relax both the non-satiation condition and the condition that in each price and income situation a unique commodity bundle is purchased. Even if more than one bundle may be chosen in any price/income situation and if there exist points at which not all income is spent we can still in certain conditions deduce the existence of a transitive preference ordering in which the consumer can be taken as maximising. Richter replaces the strong axiom of revealed preference by the *congruence axiom*, which has its force in situations in which more than one commodity bundle is chosen. Thus let $h(\mathbf{p}, M)$ be the collection of all commodity bundles $\mathbf{x}$ which are chosen in the situation $(\mathbf{p}, M)$. Then the congruence axiom states that if $\mathbf{x}$ is in the collection $h(\mathbf{p}, M)$ and if there is a bundle $\mathbf{y}$ such that $\Sigma p_i y_i \leqslant M$ and $\mathbf{x} Q \mathbf{y}$ then $\mathbf{y}$ is in the collection $h(\mathbf{p}, M)$.

In words, the consumer is 'congruous' if the collection of commodity bundles chosen in each budgetary situation consists exactly of feasible bundles which can be directly or indirectly revealed preferred to every other commodity bundle chosen in this situation. If the consumer is congruous and if all non-negative price and income situations are considered and if every non-negative bundle is chosen in some price and income situation, then Richter shows that, subject to some technical conditions, there exists a utility function that the consumer can be taken as maximising, although the indifference curves corresponding to the utility function may not be strictly convex to the origin but may have linear segments or points of absolute satiation. The congruence axiom is considerably weaker than the strong axiom of revealed preference since we do not require uniqueness of the bundle chosen at each price/income situation. If we have non-satiation then it can be shown that if the strong axiom of revealed preference holds then the weak axiom holds, but on the other hand if the congruence axiom holds the weak axiom may not hold. It is, however, clear that since we can deduce the existence of a utility function from the congruence axiom, we can deduce the conclusions of traditional demand theory from this axiom.

INTEGRABILITY

The problem of integrability is historically much older than the development of the revealed preference approach and can be analysed independently of it. Suppose we are given a system of smooth demand functions $x_i = f^i(\mathbf{p}, M)$ which have the property that if all prices and income are doubled then the purchases x_i are unchanged. Then under what conditions is it possible to show that the existence of the system of demand functions implies that there exists an indifference map which is reflected in the demand functions? We do not necessarily require that the indifference map have the properties of strict convexity to the origin but we do require non-satiation. The problem as framed is essentially a purely mathematical point, and to avoid as much technicality as possible only a rather broad outline of the problem will be given. Suppose we are given the smooth system of demand functions

$$x_i = f^i(\mathbf{p}, M)$$

defined for all non-negative prices and positive incomes. Since the quantities demanded are unchanged when prices and income are changed proportionally, we can multiply prices and income by any number and leave the quantities unchanged. So multiplying by $1/M$ we have

$$x_i = f^i(\mathbf{p}, M) = f^i\left(\frac{1}{M}\mathbf{p}, 1\right) = h^i\left(\frac{1}{M}\mathbf{p}\right)$$

so that we have a system of demand functions which depends only on the ratio of prices to income. We want to find conditions under which this system of demand functions can be treated as if they were derived from maximising a utility function $u(x_1 \ldots x_n)$. We can in fact do this in two stages since we know that if there were to exist a utility function $u(x_1 \ldots x_n)$ we could express it in indirect form as $v[(1/M)\mathbf{p}] = v(\mathbf{q})$ where $q_i = (1/M)p_i$. Then around a 'price indifference' curve of $v(q)$ along which v is constant the equation

$$\sum_i \frac{\partial v(\mathbf{q})}{\partial q_i} \, \mathrm{d}q_i = 0$$

would hold.

We wish to show that under certain conditions such a function $v(\mathbf{q})$ exists, and in order to do this it is convenient to start from the equation

$$\sum_{i=1}^{n} x_i(\mathbf{q}) \, \mathrm{d}q_i = 0$$

The problem is then to identify the conditions under which, for suitable paths of prices, the demand functions can be interpreted as partial derivatives of some function $v(q)$. Suppose that we fix any two points $\mathbf{q}_0\,\mathbf{q}_1$ and consider all paths of the q_i which link up $\mathbf{q}_0$ and $\mathbf{q}_1$. Then we could describe movements along any of these paths by a sequence of values of $(\mathrm{d}q_1 \ldots \mathrm{d}q_n)$ telling us in which direction to move from one point to the next on the path. Remembering that each of the x_i depend on the $(q_1 \ldots q_n)$, as the q_i change moving along any path between $\mathbf{q}_0$ and $\mathbf{q}_1$, so the x_i will also change. If we then consider the above equation we are really picking out those paths of movement of the $(q_1 \ldots q_n)$ between $\mathbf{q}_0$ and $\mathbf{q}_1$ along which at every point the equation is satisfied. If the movements satisfying this equation between two points are to represent movements along a 'price indifference' curve then we know that the sum of the values of the expressions $\Sigma x_i \, dq_i$ along the whole length of each path must be the same irrespective of which particular path satisfying the equation is selected.

To illustrate this requirement we use Fig. 28; consider the special case in which $\mathbf{q}_0 = \mathbf{q}_1$ so that we are considering all

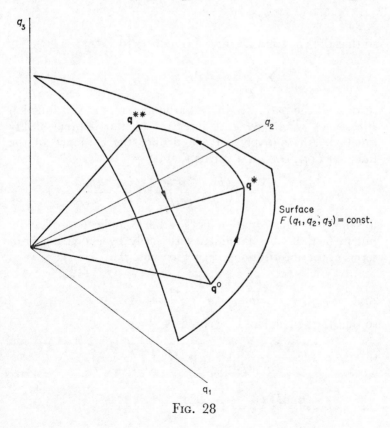

FIG. 28

paths to and from $\mathbf{q}_0$ such that at every point on the path $\Sigma x_i \, dq_i = 0$. One such path is to move from $\mathbf{q}^0$ to $\mathbf{q}^*$, then to $\mathbf{q}^{**}$ and so back to $\mathbf{q}^0$, while another is obviously to remain stationary at $\mathbf{q}^0$. In general the sum of the values of the $\Sigma x_i \, dq_i$ will vary with different paths, but if our movements are to reflect movements around a price indifference curve then all of these paths must give rise to the same value of the sum of $\Sigma x_i \, dq_i$ since in effect this value will be the constant value of the utility level of the 'price indifference' curve. There are several ways of expressing mathematically the conditions under which this is true: if the value along any path is to be the same then there must exist some function $F(q_1 \ldots q_n)$ such that

$$x_i(q_1 \ldots q_n) = \theta \, \frac{\partial F(q_1 \ldots q_n)}{\partial q_i}$$

so that the equation $\Sigma x_i \, dq_i = 0$ reduces to

$$\theta \sum \frac{\partial F}{\partial q_i} \, dq_i = dF(q_1 \ldots q_n) = 0$$

so that all the paths are indeed around contours of a function $F(q_1 \ldots q_n)$ which we can interpret as the indirect utility function. Alternatively we can deduce the existence of the function $F(q_1 \ldots q_n)$ if it is true that

$$x_k \left(\frac{\partial x_i}{\partial q_j} - \frac{\partial x_j}{\partial q_i} \right) + x_i \left(\frac{\partial x_j}{\partial q_k} - \frac{\partial x_k}{\partial q_j} \right) + x_j \left(\frac{\partial x_k}{\partial q_i} - \frac{\partial x_i}{\partial q_k} \right) = 0$$

for all i, j, k. This equation looks rather complicated to handle but in fact can be simplified very easily by expressing it in terms of the substitution effect. First note that

$$\frac{\partial x_i}{\partial p_j} = \frac{\partial x_i}{\partial q_j} \frac{\partial q_j}{\partial p_j} = \frac{\partial x_i}{\partial q_j} \frac{1}{M}$$

so that the system can be written as

$$0 = x_k(\mathbf{p}, M) \left(\frac{\partial x_i}{\partial p_j} - \frac{\partial x_j}{\partial p_i} \right) + x_i(\mathbf{p}, M) \left(\frac{\partial x_j}{\partial p_k} - \frac{\partial x_k}{\partial p_j} \right)$$

$$+ x_j(\mathbf{p}, M) \left(\frac{\partial x_k}{\partial p_i} - \frac{\partial x_i}{\partial p_k} \right)$$

Remembering that

$$\frac{\delta x_i}{\delta p_j} = \frac{\partial x_i}{\partial p_j} + x_j \frac{\partial x_i}{\partial M}$$

and similarly for goods j, k and prices i, k, the equation reduces to

$$x_k \left| \frac{\delta x_i}{\delta p_j} - \frac{\delta x_j}{\delta p_i} \right| + x_i \left| \frac{\delta x_j}{\delta p_k} - \frac{\delta x_k}{\delta p_j} \right| + x_j \left| \frac{\delta x_k}{\delta p_i} - \frac{\delta x_i}{\delta p_k} \right| = 0$$

which can hold for all values of x_i, x_j, x_k, only if $\delta x_i/\delta p_j = \delta x_i/\delta p_j$ for all i and j. Hence if every pair of substitution effects is symmetric, then we can deduce that there exists a function $F(p_1 \ldots p_n, M)$ which we may locally at least interpret as the indirect utility function.

We now have two sets of conditions: symmetry of the substitution effects, and Houthakker's strong axiom of revealed preference, sufficient to allow us to deduce the existence of a function which we can interpret as a utility function, at least locally. In the revealed preference approach the contours of this function will be strictly convex to the origin but in the pure integrability case, using only symmetry of the substitution effects, we can deduce the existence of smooth contours, but we need to introduce some additional conditions of the form that

$$\sum_{i,j} p_i p_j \frac{\delta x_i}{\delta p^j} \leqslant 0$$

to ensure that the contours are convex rather than concave to the origin. It is also worth pointing out that if there are only two goods and hence only two demand functions then solely from a knowledge of the demand functions we can always deduce the existence of a function $v(x_1, x_2)$ which can be interpreted as a utility function. This follows from the fact that the budget constraint must hold and that if all prices and income are doubled then the quantities demanded remain unchanged. Indeed it is possible to deduce [37] from these facts that, with only two goods, the substitution effects

$$\frac{\partial x_i}{\partial p_j} + x_j \frac{\partial x_i}{\partial M}$$

C

must be symmetric. The intuition is that only the price ratio p_2/p_1 and the income level M affect the quantities demanded of the two goods. If, however, we fix two price ratios and consider all movements of price ratios between these two points which satisfy an equation stating that the implicit utility level should remain constant, then there is in fact only a single such path of price change. Hence the sums of the values of consumption changes cannot vary with the path selected and hence no additional condition is needed to ensure integrability. Thus in the two good case it is always possible, so long as the demand functions are smooth, to deduce the existence of a function which could be interpreted as a utility function.

How then in the end is it possible to interpret the problem of integrability and the approach of revealed preference analysis? We have shown that it is possible to define restrictions on an arbitrary collection of demand functions which are in principle testable and which are sufficient to allow us to deduce that the demand functions can be interpreted as if they were derived from a utility function. We can also deduce properties about market behaviour from the restrictions on choice behaviour entirely analogous to those deduced by starting directly with the utility function rather than with observed market behaviour. Hence the two approaches to analysing choice behaviour are ultimately equivalent: each implies the other. We should then be guided when solving actual problems into using that approach which is the more natural for the problem on hand. In particular, traditional methods depend more heavily than the revealed preference approach on non-satiation and on positive consumption of every good, which suggests that revealed preference analysis may be more useful for studying these types of situation.

4 The Structure of Preference Orderings

INTRODUCTION

Any consumer satisfying the postulates of demand theory will act as if he were endowed with a demand function for each good. Clearly in any system of demand functions there is a very large amount of information, and to derive all of this information and hence the demand functions from published statistics of quantities purchased, prices and income is a very difficult task. Historically economists have sought to facilitate the problem by summarising the information through grouping goods together when they display similar roles in consumer behaviour. One natural line of approach is to consider the extent to which pairs of goods complement one another, or are rivals for each other in consumer tastes. Thus two goods are defined as *complements* if, whenever the consumption of one increases in some way, the consumption of the other also increases. The two goods are *substitutes* if the opposite is the case. It is worth noting that an essential aspect of complementarity relations is that only pairs of goods are considered. However, if in any situation there are n goods, then the relationships between any pair of goods will, in general, depend at least partly on the consumer's choices with respect to each of the other $(n-2)$ goods. Hence we should be a little sceptical of the generality of definitions involving only pairs of goods. Nevertheless instances can be imagined where such definitions provide a useful means of summarising the information provided within a system of demand functions. Thus suppose that competition in markets tends to ensure that suppliers charge equal or near-equal prices in every situation for pairs of goods that are close substitutes. Then as Hicks has pointed out [31], since the prices of substitutes vary proportionately, we can aggregate the two substitutes together to form a single good in the demand functions using the fixed price ratio as weights.

In slightly more detail, we can easily demonstrate that if there is a group of goods each of whose prices vary proportionally, then we can find a single aggregate price and quantity measure representing the price and quantity of the group such that whenever the original utility function is maximised subject to the original budget constraint then a utility function expressed in terms of the aggregate quantity is maximised subject to a budget constraint expressed in terms of the aggregate quantity and the aggregate price. Thus suppose we are given the utility function $u(\mathbf{x}_1, \mathbf{x}_2)$ where $\mathbf{x}_2$ is a group of goods whose prices $\mathbf{p}_2$ always vary proportionally. This means that there exist some base period prices $\mathbf{p}_2^0$ and a constant θ such that $\mathbf{p}_2 = \theta\mathbf{p}_2^0$. Then we can define an aggregate quantity X_2, a number, an aggregate price p for the quantity X_2, and a utility function $v(\mathbf{x}_1, X_2)$ such that if $u(\mathbf{x}_1, \mathbf{x}_2)$ is maximised subject to the budget constraint

$$\sum_{i=1}^{k} p_i x_i + \sum_{i=k+1}^{n} p_i x_i = M$$

then $v(\mathbf{x}_1, X_2)$ is maximised subject to the budget constraint $\sum_{=1}^{k} p_i x_i + p X_2 = M$ where

$$\mathbf{x}_1 = (x_1, \ldots, x_k)$$
$$\mathbf{x}_2 = (x_{k+1}, \ldots, x_n)$$

Indeed, let

$$X_2 = \sum_{i=k+1}^{n} p_i^0 x_i \qquad p = \theta$$

and let $v(\mathbf{x}_1, X_2) = \text{Max}\left\{u(\mathbf{x}_1, \mathbf{x}_2) \,\middle|\, \sum_{i=k+1}^{n} p_i^0 x_i = X_2\right\}$ for a fixed value of X_2 and of $\mathbf{x}_1$. We have to show that whenever the optimising necessary conditions

$$\frac{u_i}{u_j} = \frac{p_i}{p_j} \quad \text{and} \quad \sum_{i=1}^{k} p_i x_i + \sum_{i=k+1}^{n} p_i x_i = M$$

hold, then the aggregate optimising necessary conditions

$$\frac{v_i}{vX_2} = \frac{p_i}{p} = 1,\ldots, k \quad \text{and} \quad \sum_{i=1}^{k} p_i x_i + pX_2 = M$$

also hold. If

$$\sum_{i=1}^{k} p_i x_i + \sum_{i=k+1}^{n} p_i x_i = M$$

then obviously

$$\sum_{i=1}^{k} p_i x_i + pX_2 = M$$

since

$$pX_2 = \theta \sum_{i=k+1}^{n} p_i^0 x_i = \sum_{i=k+1}^{n} p_i x_i$$

On the other hand since

$$\text{Max}_{x_2}\left\{ u(\mathbf{x}_1, \mathbf{x}_2) \,\middle|\, \sum_{i=k+1}^{n} p_i^0 x_i = X_2 \right\}$$

$$= \text{Max}_{x_2}\left\{ u(x_1, x_2) \,\middle|\, \theta \sum_{k+1}^{n} p_i^0 x_i = \theta X_2 \right\}$$

$$= \text{Max}_{x_2}\left\{ u(x_1, x_2) \,\middle|\, \sum_{i=k+1}^{n} p_i x_i = M - \sum_{i=1}^{k} p_i x_i \right\}$$

we have the result that, maximising u over all $(\mathbf{x}_1, \mathbf{x}_2)$ satisfying the overall budget constraint, is equivalent to first maximising u over $\mathbf{x}_2$ which involves exactly the optimal expenditure on the second group and then using the balance of income to maximise over $\mathbf{x}_1$. Hence whenever the overall problem is solved, then $v(\mathbf{x}_1, X_2)$ must be maximised over all $(\mathbf{x}_1, X_2)$ satisfying

$$\sum_{i=1}^{k} p_i x_i + pX_2 = M.$$

Hence we can reduce the group $\mathbf{x}_2$ to a single good X_2 with a price θ for purposes of demand analysis [62].

MEASURES OF SUBSTITUTES AND COMPLEMENTS

Various alternative formal definitions have been proposed to express the intuitive content of substitute/complement relationships. The aim is to find summary measures expressed in terms of the observable properties of demand functions which reflect the relationships in consumer preferences between varying quantities of different goods. Examples might be petrol and cars on the one hand and cake and biscuits on the other hand. Most consumers (other than motor museum owners!) will tend either to purchase both cars and petrol or neither while for many consumers either cake or biscuits might be purchased depending on their relative prices, the consumer's income and no doubt, many other factors. There seems to be some force in the argument that it is unrealistic to expect to be able to define a single simple observable measure which adequately reflects the relationships between any pair of goods in satisfying the needs of the consumer as expressed in his preference ordering and that we should instead look at the structure of the entire utility function representing his preferences (see the next section on separable utility [46, 37]). However, since various simple measures have been proposed and have also been used extensively in general equilibrium models, it is worth examining these measures. The first measure hinges on the sign of the substitution effect.

Hicks [31] suggested that goods i and j should be called complements if the substitution term

$$\frac{\delta x_i}{\delta p_j} < 0 \quad \text{and substitutes if} \quad \frac{\delta x_i}{\delta p_j} > 0$$

One difficulty which arises is that the substitution effect may change sign between different price and income situations. For an unambiguous definition, we should have to require that this never occurred. However, this measure does only depend on the indifference map and not on any cardinal property of the utility function. Moreover since for all goods the own substitution effect $\delta x_i/\delta p_i$ is always negative, the criterion expresses the intuitive concept that if goods are complements then consumption of the goods moves together to keep the utility level unchanged. However, we know that in the non-integrable case $\delta x_i/\delta p_j \neq \delta x_j/\delta p_i$ although the consumer may still have demand functions so that in this case it is possible for good i to be a complement for good j while good j is a substitute for good i. It is also true that if $\delta x_i/\delta p_j = 0$ at some price/income situation then the indifference curve has a kink at this price ratio, a case typically regarded as one of complementarity, although our measure would not reveal the pair of goods to be complements. A further implication of this measure is that, if there are only two goods then, according to this measure, they will always be substitutes: this follows immediately from the fact that demand functions are homogeneous of degree zero so that

$$\frac{\delta x_1}{\delta p_1} p_1 + \frac{\delta x_1}{\delta p_2} p_2 = 0 \text{ for all prices } (p_1, p_2)$$

which since $\delta x_1/\delta p_1 < 0$ means $\delta x_1/\delta p_2 > 0$. This is quite reasonable, since if there are only two goods, then so long as all income is spent, what is not spent on one good must be spent on the other. Hence purchases of the two goods should move in opposite directions.

With more than two goods the homogeneity of degree zero of the demand functions restricts the degree of complementarity that is possible within the system. Thus since, in general, we must always have

$$\sum_{i=1}^{n} p_i \frac{\delta x_i}{\delta p_j} = 0$$

for each good i, then at least one pair of goods must be net substitutes. In other words, since any adjustment of purchases to price changes must be within the income constraint, then not all purchases of all goods may increase in response to a price fall in one of the goods. Overall this measure appears to be reasonably satisfactory, although it still suffers from the defect that our classification of the relationships between pairs of goods depends on how the quantities of other goods changes.

An analogous measure, generally referred to as a definition of *gross complements* or *gross substitutes* to avoid confusion with the above 'net' definitions (net of income effects), uses the partial derivatives of the ordinary demand functions. A good i is a gross complement for good j if $\partial x_i/\partial p_j < 0$ and is a gross substitute if $\partial x_i/\partial p_j > 0$. Again this sign condition must be interpreted as holding at all price/income situations. Since in the general case we certainly do not have

$$\frac{\partial x_i}{\partial p_j} = \frac{\partial x_j}{\partial p_i}$$

the definition will not generally be symmetric between goods i and j. Note, however, that if goods i and j are net complements for one another then unless either of the goods is a strongly inferior good, they will also be gross complements for one another. We could also quite easily have a case where goods i and j were net substitutes but gross complements for one another. Note also that since $\partial x_i/\partial p_i$ may have any sign, it is rather difficult to interpret the condition for gross complements in terms of the consumption of two goods always moving together. The net definitions seem both to bear a closer relationship to expressing the intuitive restrictions on tastes embodied in the notions of substitutes and complements and to have fewer undesirable properties as measures than the gross concepts.

However, the gross concepts have certainly found uses in general equilibrium models and particularly in the context of the uniqueness and stability of a general equilibrium. We can also demonstrate the geometrical effect of assuming a pair of goods (i, j) to be gross substitutes. Thus in Fig. 29, the offer curve measures how the ratio x_i/x_j varies when p_i varies for p_j, M constant. Thus the slope of the offer curve is given by

$$\frac{\partial}{\partial p_i}\left(\frac{x_i}{x_j}\right) = \left[\frac{\partial x_i}{\partial p_i} - \frac{x_i}{x_j^2}\frac{\partial x_j}{\partial p_i}\right]$$

Hence if goods i and j are gross substitutes and so long as good i is not a Giffen good then the offer curve will always have a negative slope: as p_i increases from budget line **p** to **p'** the optimal ratio x_i/x_j must fall. Hence the assumption of gross substitutability prevents the offer curve 'bending back' on itself.

A further disadvantage of both the above possible definitions is that they depend on the units in which goods are measured while the sign of the above measures is obviously invariant under changes in units. If we want to deduce something about the degree of complementarity or substitutability between goods from the magnitude of the partial derivative, then we should modify our measure so that it is unit-free. This suggests that some form of elasticity measure of the indifference curves might be a natural means of reflecting the shape of the indifference curves between different pairs of goods in a region around the equilibrium point. One possibility might be the

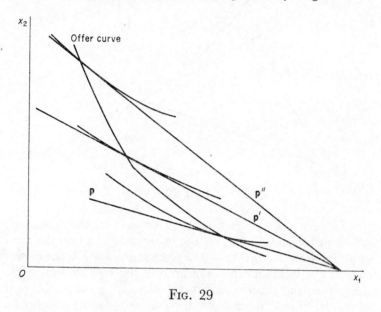

Fig. 29

elasticity of substitution between any pair of goods at the equilibrium point. Thus if we hold the level of utility constant and the quantities of all goods consumed except two constant, then we have an indifference curve. At this point we can define the *elasticity of substitution* as the percentage change in the ratio of the two goods consumed, given geometrically by the change in slope of the line from the origin to the point on the indifference curve, resulting from a 1 per cent change in the slope of the budget line. (Fig. 30). Geometrically the elasticity is given by the movement from x_i/x_j to $(x_i/x_j)'$ due to the change from $\mathbf{p}$ to $\mathbf{p}'$. This would seem to measure the curvature of the indifference curve about the equilibrium point, but note

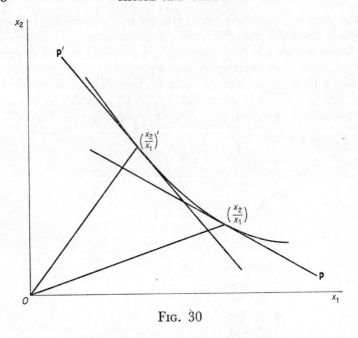

FIG. 30

that, in general, the measure will depend on the (constant)
values of consumption of all the other goods and on the level
of utility as well as on the initial price ratio. The less the curvature of the indifference curve around the equilibrium point,
the higher the substitutability relationship between the pair
of goods. Since the measure involves movements around an
indifference curve as the budget line changes, one would expect to be able to express mathematically the measure in terms
of the substitution effect parameter between the two goods.
Indeed in [46] a rather similar measure has been defined; the
degree of substitution being measured by

$$\left[\dfrac{\dfrac{\delta x_i}{\delta p_j} \dfrac{\delta x_i}{\delta p_i} - \dfrac{\delta x_j}{\delta p_j} \dfrac{\delta x_j}{\delta p_i}}{\dfrac{\delta x_j}{\delta p_j} \dfrac{\delta x_i}{\delta p_i} - \dfrac{\delta x_i}{\delta p_j} \dfrac{\delta x_j}{\delta p_i}} \right]$$

which again reflects the curvature of the indifference curve.

THE THEORY OF SEPARABLE UTILITY FUNCTIONS

A further means of summarising the information implicit in a system of demand functions lies in considering restrictions on the way in which goods are grouped together within the utility function.[1] This approach can be thought of as directly investigating the structure of the different needs of the consumer and the ways in which various goods enter into the satisfaction of those needs [26, 29, 30]. Broadly this approach, known as *separability analysis*, is concerned with the possibility of dividing up the commodity bundle into a number of sub-bundles in such a way that the level of utility afforded by a particular commodity bundle $\mathbf{x}$ depends only on the levels of satisfaction yielded by various subcollections of the given commodity bundle and on a uniform relationship between goods in different subcollections. Goods within a subcollection may bear any relationship with one another but goods from different subcollections must bear a similar relationship to one another. To expound upon this theme, some formal definitions will be helpful. Let us say that a utility function is separable if it can be written as

$$u(x_1 \ldots x_n) = \phi\{v^1(\mathbf{x}_1) \ldots v^R(\mathbf{x}_R)\}$$

and additively separable if it can be written as

$$u(x_1 \ldots x_n) = \phi\left\{ \sum_{r=1}^{R} v^r(\mathbf{x}^r) \right\}$$

where $(\mathbf{x}^1 \ldots \mathbf{x}^R)$ is a division of the n good bundle $(x_1 \ldots x_n)$ into R subgroups $\mathbf{x}_r$ such that each good belongs to only one subdivision $\mathbf{x}_r$ but every good belongs to one of the subdivisions. Thus in the first case the levels of specific satisfaction $v^r(\mathbf{x}_r)$ derived from consuming each of the subgroups of goods depends only on the quantities of these goods while in the second case not only is this true but it is also true

---

[1] The particular exposition of separable utility adopted here owes a lot to the teaching of Professor Gorman as well as to the published literature.

that the overall utility level depends only on the sum of the specific satisfaction levels. Clearly any additively separable utility function is separable but the converse does not hold. The type of situation envisaged is one where there are two stages in deriving utility from consumption; in the first stage, goods within a subgroup contribute towards a particular type of satisfaction provided by goods within the subgroup in the way that different types of food might lead to various levels of satisfaction of hunger; while in the second stage these various types of satisfaction are aggregated together to give an overall satisfaction level. We wish to explore the implications of these kinds of restrictions on tastes in at least two directions: first, what are the additional axiomatic restrictions that must be made on the individual's preference ordering (additional to those of our standard consumer) in order for the individual's preference ordering to be representable by a separable **or** additively separable utility function? Second, what are the implications of such a utility function for the demand functions and hence the market behaviour of our representative consumer?

To deal first with the nature of the preference ordering, suppose that the individual is endowed with a 'weak' preference ordering R which is representable by the continuous increasing utility function $u(x_1, \ldots, x_n)$ so that $u(x_1, \ldots, x_n) \geqslant u(y_1, \ldots, y_n)$ if and only if $(x_1, \ldots, x_n) R(y_1, \ldots, y_n)$. Let each of the possible n commodity bundles $(x_1, \ldots, x_n)$ be subdivided in the mutually exclusive and exhaustive way outlined above into R subgroups $(\mathbf{x}^1, \ldots, \mathbf{x}^R)$. As the total bundle $\mathbf{x}$ varies over all the possible bundles under consideration each sub-bundle $\mathbf{x}^r$ varies over all possible values of the given sub-bundle. Now let $\mathbf{x}^{r*}$ be the sub-bundle of goods derived by putting together all the sub-bundles except $\mathbf{x}^r$ so that $\mathbf{x}^{r*}$ is the bundle $\mathbf{x}$ except for the fact that the rth sub-bundle has been removed, i.e. $\mathbf{x}^{r*} = (\mathbf{x}^1, \ldots, \mathbf{x}^{r-1} | \mathbf{x}^{r+1}, \ldots, \mathbf{x}^R)$ and any total bundle $\mathbf{x}$ may be derived by putting together $\mathbf{x}^{r*}$ and $\mathbf{x}^r$ in an appropriate fashion $\mathbf{x} = (\mathbf{x}^{r*}, \mathbf{x}^r)$. Hence we can decompose $\mathbf{x}$ into a particular sub-bundle and all remaining sub-bundles in R ways by picking out in turn each specific sub-bundle $\mathbf{x}^r(r = 1, 2, \ldots R)$. Thus if in all there are three goods

$\mathbf{x} = (x_1, x_2, x_3)$ grouped in two groups $\mathbf{x}^1 = (x_1)$ $\mathbf{x}^2 = (x_2, x_3)$ then we can regard $\mathbf{x}$ as composed either of $(\mathbf{x}^1, \mathbf{x}^{1*})$ or $(\mathbf{x}^2, \mathbf{x}^{2*})$ where here $\mathbf{x}^{1*} = \mathbf{x}^2$ and $\mathbf{x}^1 = \mathbf{x}^{2*}$. The collection of all total bundles $\mathbf{x}$ is ordered by R by hypothesis, and the ordering R actually induces an ordering over each collection of sub-bundles in the following way. Let r be any fixed value, i.e. pick out a particular subgroup $\mathbf{x}^r$ and regard $\mathbf{x}$ as $(\mathbf{x}^r, \mathbf{x}^{r*})$. Now let $\mathbf{x}$ vary over all total bundles which always have the fixed values $\mathbf{x}^{r*}$ outside group r. Then we know that either $\mathbf{x} = (\mathbf{x}^r, \mathbf{x}^{r*})R(\mathbf{y}^r, \mathbf{x}^{r*}) = \mathbf{y}$ or $\mathbf{y}R\mathbf{x}$. Define an ordering R_r over the $\mathbf{x}^r$ in the following way: $\mathbf{x}^r R_r \mathbf{y}^r$ if and only if $(\mathbf{x}^r, \mathbf{x}^{r*})R(\mathbf{y}^r, \mathbf{x}^{r*})$. One sub-bundle is at least as good as another if the total bundles formed from the two subvectors in group r and the common sub-bundle outside group r stand in this relationship under the ordering R. Then R_r is an ordering of the $\mathbf{x}^r$ satisfying the conditions which R satisfies. Note that, as defined R_r depends on the particular $\mathbf{x}^{r*}$ chosen to be held constant since there is no guarantee that $(\mathbf{x}_r, \mathbf{x}^{r*})R(\mathbf{y}_r, \mathbf{x}^{r*})$ if and only if $(\mathbf{x}_r, \mathbf{y}^{r*})R(\mathbf{y}_r, \mathbf{y}^{r*})$ where $\mathbf{y}^{r*} \neq \mathbf{x}^{r*}$ is any other possible sub-bundle outside group r. To indicate this dependence we write R_r as $R_r(\mathbf{x}^{r*})$ and refer to it as the conditional ordering over the sub-bundles $\mathbf{x}^r$ induced by R and conditional on the particular fixed bundle $\mathbf{x}^{r*}$ that we have chosen. Next suppose that for each r the conditional preference ordering is in fact independent of $\mathbf{x}^{r*}$, i.e. $R_r(\mathbf{x}^{r*})$ is the same ordering of the $\mathbf{x}^r$ for all $\mathbf{x}^{r*}$ for each r. Then the original ordering R of total bundles $\mathbf{x}$ is said to be separable with respect to the particular grouping of goods chosen. If a preference ordering is separable, then the way in which preferences are expressed between sub-bundles of goods within a group is completely unaffected by the goods made available outside the group. Separability of R is in fact just the axiomatic restriction on preferences that we have been looking for to yield a separable utility function. Indeed it can be shown [18, 29] that a necessary and sufficient condition for the utility function representing R to be separable is that R should be separable. That this should be so is not difficult to see: if the utility function is separable then we can just use the group specific satisfaction function to define the suborderings

R_r so that $\mathbf{x}^r R_r \mathbf{y}^r$ if and only if $v^r(\mathbf{x}^r) \geqslant v^r(\mathbf{y}^r)$. Since $\phi(v^1 \ldots v^R)$ is increasing in each v^r, i.e. if v^r increases with all other vs held constant, then ϕ increases, this subordering R_r satisfies our definition of a subordering and is also clearly independent of goods consumed outside the rth group. On the other hand, if the ordering R is separable then choices within each group can be considered independently of choices in other groups and so a subutility function $v^r(\mathbf{x}^r)$ can be defined representing each subordering R^r and $\phi(.)$ defined in a consistent fashion to yield the overall utility level. At a more fundamental level the link between the two concepts is quite clear: separable utility means that the marginal rate of substitution between goods within a group, and hence consumer choices, should depend only on goods within the group, which is exactly the same restriction laid down by separability of the preference ordering R.

To consider the same question in the case of additively separable utility functions, it is quite clear that we will have to lay down stronger restrictions on R than separability with respect to a given grouping of the goods since not every separable utility function is additively separable. To proceed we have to introduce the notion of an *overgrouping*: suppose that the subdivision of the n goods into R groups $[1, 2 \ldots R]$ is given so that $\mathbf{x} = (\mathbf{x}^1 \ldots \mathbf{x}^R)$. Then any way of reducing the number of groups to $R' \leqslant R$ putting two or more of the groups together to form a single larger group is called an overgrouping. Thus if there are three groups $(1, 2, 3)$ then all possible overgroupings can be derived by putting two or more of the groups together in the following ways:

$$(1, [23]) \quad (2, [13]) \quad (3, [12]) \quad ([123]) \quad (1, 2, 3)$$

The number of possible overgroupings depends on the number of groups originally distinguished. The restriction on preferences that we are looking for is that the preference ordering R should be separable with respect to each possible overgrouping of the groups into $(1', 2' \ldots R')$ with the exception of the extreme case where all groups are combined into a single overgrouping $(1')$ and also that R should be separable with respect to the original subdivision $(1 \ldots R)$. This is clearly much stronger than separability of R and in fact it can be shown that so long as the number of individual goods is at least three (since with only two goods it is easy to see that any ordering R satisfies conditions both for separability and additive separability) then the utility function representing R is additively separable if and only if R satisfies the above conditions. The reason for this can be fairly easily demonstrated with an example involving only three groups. Since for each over-grouping R is separable, we know that for each overgrouping a separable utility function exists. Hence we have the following equations, corresponding to each possible overgrouping,

$$
\begin{aligned}
u(\mathbf{x}^1, \mathbf{x}^2, \mathbf{x}^3) &= \phi^1 \{v^{11}(\mathbf{x}^1), v^{12}(\mathbf{x}^2\,\mathbf{x}^3)\} \\
&= \phi^2 \{v^{21}(\mathbf{x}^2), v^2(\mathbf{x}^1\,\mathbf{x}^3)\} \\
&= \phi^3 \{v^{31}(\mathbf{x}^3), v^{32}(\mathbf{x}^1\,\mathbf{x}^2)\} \\
&= \phi \{v^1(\mathbf{x}^1), v^2(\mathbf{x}^2), v^3(\mathbf{x}^3)\}
\end{aligned}
$$

From this, it is clear that whatever the form of $\phi(.)$ it must treat each of the three subgroups in exactly the same way since we have to be able to achieve the same result regardless of the positioning of a certain subgroup. If $\phi(v^1, v^2, v^3)$ actually has the form $\psi(v^1 + v^2 + v^3)$ then each group is treated in the same way and in fact it happens to be true that addition is the only form of ϕ that will satisfy our requirements [29]. If the function form is additive, then in a sense where we put each group makes no difference. While we have only illustrated the argument for three groups it is in fact true for any number of groups.

We should also note that there are more general possibilities than the structure of the utility function outlined above. Thus it may be that the preference ordering R is not itself separable but that it is separable when a given subvector of goods is included within each of the subgroups. This leads us to examine, as a straightforward generalisation of the above, utility functions of the form

$$
u(x_1, \ldots, x_n, y_1, \ldots, y_p) = \phi \{v^1(\mathbf{x}^1, \mathbf{y}) \ldots v^R(\mathbf{x}^R, \mathbf{y})\}
$$

where $(y_1, \ldots, y_p) = \mathbf{y}$ is some sub-bundle included in each of the groups. In the same way we may have a combination of separable and additively separable choices so that groups

$(1,\ldots, P)$ are additive while groups $(P+1,\ldots, R)$ are just separable. This leads to a utility function of the form

$$u(x_1\ldots x_n) = \phi\left[\sum_{r=1}^{P} v^r(\mathbf{x}^r); \; \psi\{w'(\mathbf{x}^{P+1})\ldots w^R(\mathbf{x}^R)\} \right]$$

A further possibility might be that there are several levels of grouping so that we may be able to represent choices by a utility tree type of construction [59, 26]. Thus, for example, the utility function may be separable into two groups $(\mathbf{x}^1, \mathbf{x}^2)$ and then $\mathbf{x}^1$ may itself be additively separable into R_1 groups, each of which may in turn satisfy some separability restrictions. A simple example of a utility function of this form might be, with five goods in all,

$$u(x_1\ldots x_3) = \psi[\phi^1\{v^1(x_1) + v^2(x_2 x_3)\}; \; \phi^2(x_4 x_5)]$$

This type of multilevel structure has found application in for example [44], where the grouping of goods at different levels reflects the varying kinds of gaps in the substitution or complement relationships between goods.

So far this discussion of the meaning of a separable indifference map has been at a fairly abstract level. We can illustrate the theory by reference to a simple example which should help to convey the intuitive content of the concept. Thus suppose that we have only three goods (x_1, x_2, x_3) and that the first two goods are separable from the third so that the utility function describing the indifference map can be written in the form

$$u(x_1, x_2, x_3) = \phi\{v^1(x_1, x_2), v^2(x_3)\}$$

and the marginal rate of substitution between the first two goods,

$$\frac{\partial u}{\partial x_1} \Big/ \frac{\partial u}{\partial x_2} = \frac{\partial \phi}{\partial v^1} \frac{\partial v^1}{\partial x_1} \Big/ \frac{\partial \phi}{\partial v^1} \frac{\partial v^1}{\partial x_2}$$

depends only on the quantity of x_1, x_2. We can represent this situation quite simply as shown in Fig. 31.

If we keep the quantities of the first two goods fixed at any point A in the diagram but vary the quantity of the third good along the line AB, then we move from one three-dimensional indifference curve $\alpha\beta\gamma$ to another $\alpha'\beta'\gamma'$. But because of the

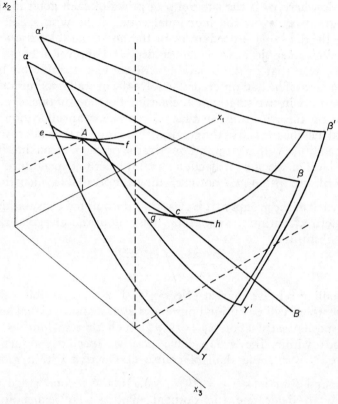

FIG. 31

separability assumption at every point such as C on the new indifference curve the marginal rate of substitution between the first two goods must be the same as at A. Geometrically this is shown by requiring the slope of the line ef to equal that of the line gh. Note that this is a definite restriction on the shapes of different indifference curves which must hold for all starting points A and all points such as C along lines such as AB.

The next task is to examine the implications for market behaviour of the consumer of a preference ordering of this kind. Suppose then that the individual has a separable utility function and faces fixed prices $(p_1 \ldots p_n) = (\mathbf{p}_1 \ldots \mathbf{p}_R)$ for goods where $\mathbf{p}_r$ is the subgroup of prices of each good in the subgroup $\mathbf{x}_r$. Now the individual could, if he wishes, follow exactly the same procedure as in the non-separable case and maximise ϕ subject to a budget constraint. However, it happens to be true that in the separable case we can describe his behaviour as if he had proceeded to solve the overall maximisation procedure in two stages: first, choosing the amount of expenditure on the rth group so that m_r represents an allocation of total income to each of the goods within group r; then allocating expenditure within groups. Consider the problem of maximising the level of specific satisfaction $v^r(\mathbf{x}_r)$ subject to expenditure on the rth group $\sum_i p_{ri} x_{ri}$ not exceeding the available allocation, for each of the groups r. It is clear that the optimal consumption pattern $\mathbf{x}_r^*$ within the rth group must entail the marginal rate of substitution

$$\frac{\partial v^r(\mathbf{x}_r^*)}{\partial x_{ri}} \bigg/ \frac{\partial v^r(\mathbf{x}_r^*)}{\partial x_{rj}}$$

equalling relative market prices p_i/p_j. For each possible value of m_r there will be optimal purchases $\mathbf{x}^r$ and an associated level of specific satisfaction $v_r^* = v^r(\mathbf{x}_r^*)$ such that so long as all goods within the group have positive specific satisfaction $\sum_i p_{ri} x_{ri}^* = m_r$. We shall of course also derive within group demand functions $x_{ri} = f^{ri}(\mathbf{p}_r, m_r)$. In the second stage we wish to determine the optimal allocation of expenditure between groups by solving the problem

Maximise $\qquad \phi\{v^1(\mathbf{x}_1) \ldots v^R(\mathbf{x}^R)\}$

subject to $\qquad x_{ri} = f^{ri}(\mathbf{p}_r, m_r) \quad (r = 1 \ldots R)$

$$\sum_{r=1}^{R} m_r = m$$

The consumer has to maximise

$$\phi[v^1\{\mathbf{F}^1(\mathbf{p}_1, m_1)\} v^2 \{\mathbf{F}^2(\mathbf{p}_2, m_2)\} \ldots v^R\{\mathbf{F}^R(\mathbf{p}^R, m_R)\}]$$

over all possible allocations of expenditure to the different groups which just exhaust income, M. This yields optimal values m_r^* of group expenditure as functions of all prices and income: $m_r^* = m_r(\mathbf{p}, M)$ where m_r^* depends on $\mathbf{p}$ since all prices enter the utility function as prices through the demand functions. This second stage in the process ensures that the marginal rate of substitution between groups is equated to relative prices, since if this were not so then expenditure could be reallocated amongst the groups to yield a higher value of overall utility ϕ. Thus the individual in this case can either be represented as solving the complete programme in a single calculation, or as if he had decided how much money to spend on each broad category of goods, leaving the detailed within-group allocation to a second-stage optimisation. We have also shown that the system of demand functions corresponding to a separable utility function can be written out 'in two stages' as

$$x_{ri} = f^{ri}(\mathbf{p}_r, m_r)$$
$$m_r = m_r(\mathbf{p}, M)$$

We can use these forms of the demand functions to derive the behavioural implications of separable utility in a rather simple fashion [49, 37].

Since the exposition of the market implications of separable utility which follow is rather technical, it is worth summarising the content of the argument by appeal to a simple three-dimensional illustration. Thus suppose again that there are three goods in quantities (x_1, x_2, x_3) and that the third is separable from the first two. The position can be summarised as is shown in Fig. 32, where the point A represents the initial position in a given price and income situation. The point γ represents consumption of goods one and two in the initial position. If there is a change in income with all prices constant, then optimal consumption plans shift along the direction of the line AB. This corresponds to a change in the consumption of goods one and two in the direction $\gamma\beta$. Note that these directions of change arise from infinitesimal income variations and so can be represented diagrammatically by straight lines. If the price of the third good changes, with income varying to compensate the consumer, then consumption of all three goods is assumed to vary in the direction αA which has a corresponding directional change of consumption of the first two goods alone of $\gamma\delta$. Thus the slope of the line $\gamma\beta$ represents the value of $(\partial x_1/\partial M)/(\partial x_2/\partial M)$ while the slope of the line $\gamma\delta$ represents the value of $(\delta x_1/\delta p_3)/(\delta x_2/\delta p_3)$ where both of these ratios are

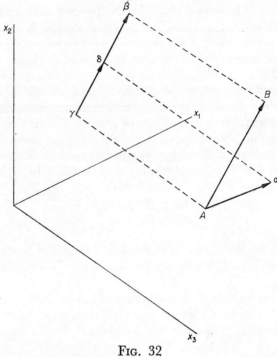

Fig. 32

evaluated at the initial price/income situation. We know that
at points A and B the marginal rate of substitution between
goods one and two (MRS_{12}) is equal, since A and B must be
points on an Engel curve corresponding to the original prices.
Similarly we know that MRS_{12} must be the same at A and α,
since at each point marginal rates of substitution are equal to
the relevant price ratio, but only the price of the third good has
changed between A and α. We also know that by separability
MRS_{12} is equal at points α and δ; at points β and B and at points
A and γ, since each of these pairs of points involve constant co-
ordinates of the first two goods. From these statements we de-
duce that MRS_{12} must be equal at points γ, δ and β so that the
point δ must be on the 'Engel curve' corresponding to the direc-
tion $\gamma\beta$. But this means that the directions $\gamma\delta$ and $\gamma\beta$ must coincide for the infinitesimal variations that we are making and so

$$\frac{\partial x_1/\partial M}{\partial x_2/\partial M} = \frac{\delta x_1/\delta p_3}{\delta x_2/\delta p_3}$$

The more mathematical argument which follows is concerned with deducing a formula rather like this as the restriction which must hold if there is a separable utility function. In fact the main restriction lies in the form of the substitution effect between groups, and so we shall find it very useful to consider the change in purchases of x_i where i is in group r arising from a change in the price of good j where j is in a group s $(s \neq r)$ when expenditure m_r on the rth group changes in a way to leave the consumer on his original indifference curve and just compensate him for the price change. We have

$$\frac{\delta x_i}{\delta p_j} = \frac{\partial x_i}{\partial p_j} + x_j \frac{\partial x_i}{\partial M}$$

However, since $x_i = f^{ri}(p_r m_r)$ any effect on x_i of a change in p_j where j is in a group different to i must be channelled through a change in m_r. Hence

$$\frac{\partial x_i}{\partial p_j} = \frac{\partial x_i}{\partial m_r} \frac{\partial m_r}{\partial p_j}$$

Also we have for similar reasons that

$$\frac{\partial x_i}{\partial m} = \frac{\partial x_i}{\partial m_r} \frac{\partial m_r}{\partial M}$$

and so

$$\frac{\delta x_i}{\delta p_j} = \left(\frac{\partial m_r}{\partial p_j} + x_j \frac{\partial m_r}{\partial M} \right) \frac{\partial x_i}{\partial m_r}$$

This equation has a very natural interpretation: the compensating change in income necessary due to a change in p_j is exactly $x_j \, dp_j$ since with this increment of income the consumer can afford but only just afford to purchase the original bundle at the new prices. Hence $\delta M / \delta p_j = x_j$ and we may rewrite our equation as

$$\frac{\delta x_i}{\delta p_j} = \left(\frac{\partial m_r}{\partial p_j} + \frac{\delta m_r}{\delta p_j} \right) \frac{\partial x_i}{\partial m_r}$$

so that the effect on purchases of x_i due to a compensated change in p_j channelled through m_r are the sum of the direct effect of the compensation on m_r and the indirect effect of the price change in changing the optimal allocation of expenditure between groups. We may also rewrite this as

$$\frac{\delta x_i}{\delta p_j} = \left[\frac{\{(\partial m_r/\partial p_j) + x_j (\partial m_r/\partial M)\}}{(\partial m_r/\partial M) \ (\partial x_j/\partial M)} \right] \frac{\partial x_i}{\partial M} \cdot \frac{\partial x_j}{\partial M}$$

$$= \lambda^{r, \, s, \, j} \frac{\partial x_i}{\partial M} \cdot \frac{\partial x_j}{\partial M}$$

where $\lambda^{r, \, s, \, j}$ is the expression in square brackets and depends on all prices and income and on the particular groups r, s and the particular price j in the jth group selected. In exactly the same way by reversing the roles of goods i and j we have

$$\frac{\delta x_j}{\delta p_i} = \lambda^{s, \, r, \, i} \frac{\partial x_j}{\partial M} \cdot \frac{\partial x_i}{\partial M}$$

and this pair of expressions must be true for any two different groups r, s and any pair of goods within these groups. From our general theory we also know that the substitution effects are symmetric and so we have

$$\frac{\delta x_i}{\delta p_j} \Big/ \frac{\partial x_i}{\partial M} \cdot \frac{\partial x_j}{\partial M} = \lambda^{r, \, s, \, j} = \lambda^{s, \, r, \, i} = \frac{\delta x_j}{\delta p_i} \Big/ \frac{\partial x_i}{\partial M} \cdot \frac{\partial x_j}{\partial M}$$

for all $r \neq s$ and all i in group r and j in group s. The next stage in the argument depends on the way in which this equation depends on the goods involved and the groups to which they belong. If we choose a good $k \neq j$ which is in group s, then we have

$$\frac{\delta x_i}{\delta p_k} \Big/ \frac{\partial x_k}{\partial M} \cdot \frac{\partial x_i}{\partial M} = \lambda^{r, \, s, \, k} = \lambda^{s, \, r, \, i} = \frac{\delta x_k}{\delta p_i} \Big/ \frac{\partial x_k}{\partial M} \cdot \frac{\partial x_i}{\partial M}$$

and so we deduce that for any and all $j \neq k$ in group s

$$\lambda^{r, \, s, \, k} = \lambda^{r, \, s, \, j}$$

In the same way if we choose a good $l \neq i$ in group r we have

$$\frac{\delta x_l}{\delta p_j} \Big/ \frac{\partial x_l}{\partial M} \cdot \frac{\partial x_j}{\partial M} = \lambda^{r, \, s, \, j} = \lambda^{s, \, r, \, l} = \frac{\delta x_j}{\delta p} \Big/ \frac{\partial x_l}{\partial M} \cdot \frac{\partial x_j}{\partial M}$$

and so

$$\lambda^{s, \, r, \, l} = \lambda^{s, \, r, \, i}$$

Hence the function λ does not actually depend on the particular goods selected within groups r and s since its value must be the same whatever the pair of goods chosen, and we can write

$$\frac{\delta x_i}{\delta p_i} = \lambda^{rs} \frac{\partial x_i}{\partial M} \frac{\partial x_i}{\partial M}$$

for all $r \neq s$ and all i in group r and j in group s. Then, since

$$\frac{\delta x_i}{\delta p_j} = \frac{\delta x_j}{\delta p_i}$$

we also know that $\lambda^{rs} = \lambda^{sr}$

Thus if the utility function is separable we have the interesting conclusion that the substitution effect between two goods belonging to different groups is equal to some function which depends only on the groups to which the two goods belong, multiplied by the product of the income terms. Separability of the utility function imposes a certain uniformity in the relations between goods belonging to different groups. If no goods belonging to two groups are inferior goods (so that the income terms are all positive) then all goods in the two groups must stand in the same net substitute relationship between groups. This restriction has also clearly reduced the amount of information in the system of demand functions: all the between-group partial derivatives $\partial x_i / \partial p_j$ where goods i and j belong to different groups are automatically known as soon as we know the income terms for every good and the terms λ^{rs}. If we tried to find a system of demand functions compatible with some published statistics of consumption of each good in different price/income situations, then if we are prepared to assume that the underlying demand functions correspond to a separable utility function, we have to estimate far fewer partial derivatives to characterise the system. Since the number of partial derivatives that can be estimated depends partly on the number of observations available in the published statistics, this is a great help.

In the case of an additively separable utility function, we would expect to get stronger restrictions on the system of demand functions, due to the fact that not only do goods fall into groups, but each group enters the utility function in a symmetrical way. If each group has the same kind of effect as every other on the level of utility, then we would expect the λ^{rs} to be the same for any two groups r and s and so to be independent of r and s. In fact this can fairly easily be shown to be true [37] and so in the additively separable case we have the between group substitution effect proportional to the product of the relevant income terms with the factor of proportionality being the same across all groups; i.e.

$$\frac{\delta x_i}{\delta p_j} = \lambda \frac{\partial x_i}{\partial M} \frac{\partial x_j}{\partial M}$$

for i and j in any two different groups. How can the λ be interpreted? Comparison of the left-hand and right-hand sides shows that the left-hand side is measured in quantity per price while the right-hand is, apart from λ, in terms of the inverse of the product of the prices, since income has the dimension of price multiplied by quantity. Hence, for consistency, λ must be some term measured in units of price multiplied by quantity. On the other hand the economics of the question is that the slope of the indifference curve in the (ij) plane is related to the slope of the expansion path at the same point, since the slope of the expansion path is just the ratio of the income terms. Movement along the expansion path involves moving from one indifference curve to another, and hence changes in the level of utility so that we might expect λ to represent some kind of utility deflator. In fact it can be shown that λ is just the negative of the ratio of the marginal utility of income to the rate of change of the marginal utility of income with respect to income [35]. As such it represents a utility deflator to allow comparisons between quantity changes for a constant utility level and quantity changes along the expansion path.

SOME EXAMPLES OF SEPARABLE UTILITY FUNCTIONS

Now that we have come this far at a fairly general level it is worth examining a few specific examples of the applications of the theory. A famous case is a simplification of Stone's linear expenditure system [58]. Suppose that there are n goods and that the utility function can be written as

$$u(x_1 \ldots x_n) = \phi\left(\sum_{i=1}^{n} a_i \log x_i \right)$$

where $\phi(.)$ is a general monotonic function. Note that in this special case each specific group satisfaction function $v^r(\mathbf{x}^r)$ has exactly the same form and that in effect there is only one good in each group, though of course, since the utility function is additively separable, we could overgroup goods in any way that we wish and preserve the form of the function. If this function is maximised subject to a given budget constraint

$$\sum_{i=1}^{n} p_i x_i = M$$

then by applying Lagrange multiplier methods, necessary conditions for a maximum are that the following $(n+1)$ equations should be satisfied by the optimal values of the $(x_1^* \ldots x_n^*)$:

$$\phi'(.) \frac{a_i}{x_i} = \lambda p_i \quad (i = 1 \ldots n)$$

$$\sum_{i=1}^{n} p_i x_i = m$$

where $\phi'(.)$ is the derivation of the function ϕ. The budget equation can be used to eliminate ϕ' and the Lagrange multiplier λ

$$\sum_{i=1}^{n} p_i x_i = \frac{\phi'(.)}{\lambda} \sum_{i=1}^{n} a_i = M$$

so that

$$\frac{\phi'}{\lambda} = \frac{M}{\sum_{i=1}^{n} a_i}$$

and the system of demand functions can be written as

$$p_i x_i = \frac{a_i}{\sum\limits_{i=1}^{n} a_i} M$$

so that expenditure on each good is a linear function of income, whence of course springs the name linear expenditure system. Notice that so long as we insist on positive marginal utility of each good everywhere, then all $a_i > 0$ and so

$$\frac{\partial x_i}{\partial M} = \frac{a_i}{\sum a_i} \frac{1}{p_i} > 0$$

for all positive prices, so that no goods are ever inferior in this system. Note also that the demand functions are dependent only on income and their own price: pairs of goods are never gross substitutes or complements. From our theory we would expect that, since there is only one good in each group, the substitution effect between any two goods will be proportional to the product of the income effects. This is in fact the case since

$$\frac{\delta x_i}{\delta p_j} = \frac{\partial x_i}{\partial p_j} + x_j \frac{\partial x_i}{\partial M} = x_j \frac{\partial x_i}{\partial M}$$

$$= \left(\frac{M}{p_j} \frac{a_j}{\sum a_k} \right) \left(\frac{a_i}{\sum a_k} \frac{1}{p_i} \right)$$

$$= \left(\frac{a_j}{\sum a_k} \frac{1}{p_j} \right) \left(\frac{a_i}{\sum a_k} \frac{1}{p_i} \right) = M \frac{\partial x_i}{\partial M} \frac{\partial x_j}{\partial M}$$

which will always be positive so that all pairs of goods are always net substitutes for one another and there is no possibility of complementarity within the system. If we define m_i as expenditure on the ith 'group', $m_i = p_i x_i$, then we can define our two stage demand functions as

$$x_i = f^i(p_i, m_i) = \frac{m_i}{p_i}$$

$$m_i = g^i(\mathbf{p}, M) = M \frac{a_i}{\sum a_i}$$

so that a constant proportion of income is spent on each good whatever the price ratios.

A second very simple case, presented purely for illustrative purposes to incidate the generality of the theory, arises when there are two groups and two goods within each group and the utility function has the form

$$u(x_1, x_2, x_3, x_4) = \phi(x_1 x_2 + x_3 x_4).$$

If this utility function is maximised subject to a budget constraint, then necessary conditions for a maximum are that the marginal rates of substitution should be equated to the relevant price ratio:

$$\frac{x_2}{x_1} = \frac{p_1}{p_2}$$

$$\frac{x_3}{x_1} = \frac{p_4}{p_2}$$

$$\sum_{i=1}^{4} p_i x_i = M$$

$$\frac{x_4}{x_1} = \frac{p_3}{p_2}$$

Then, substituting the first three equations into the budget constraint yields

$$\left(2p_i + 2\frac{p_3 p_4}{p_2}\right) x_1 = M \text{ or } x_1 = \frac{Mp_2}{2p_1 p_2 + 2p_3 p_4}$$

which in turn yields

$$x_2 = \frac{Mp_1}{(2p_1 p_2 + 2p_3 p_4)}$$

$$x_3 = \frac{Mp_4}{(2p_1 p_2 + 2p_3 p_4)}$$

$$x_4 = \frac{Mp_3}{(2p_1 p_2 + 2p_3 p_4)}$$

as the system of demand functions. If we define $m_1 = p_1 x_1 + p_2 x_2$ and $m_2 = p_3 x_3 + p_4 x_4$ then, in our two stage procedure, the demand functions may be written as

$$x_1 = f^1(p_1, p_2, m_1) = \frac{m_1}{2p_1}$$

$$x_2 = f^2(p_1, p_2, m_1) = \frac{m_1}{2p_2}$$

$$x_3 = f^3(p_3, p_4, m_2) = \frac{m_2}{2p_3}$$

$$x_4 = f^4(p_3, p_4, m_2) = \frac{m_2}{2p_4}$$

$$m_1 = g^1(\mathbf{p}, M) = \frac{2p_1 p_2 M}{2p_2 p_1 + 2p_3 p_4}$$

$$m_2 = g^2(\mathbf{p}, M) = \frac{2p_3 p_4 M}{2p_1 p_2 + 2p_3 p_4}$$

Note that a special feature of this system is that within each group an equal amount of money is spent on each good, whatever the prices; a result of the fact that the elasticity of within-group indifference curves is unity. If the substitution effects within each group and between each group are calculated then between groups pairs of goods are net complements while within groups pairs of goods are net substitutes. Thus for example

$$\frac{\delta x_2}{\delta p_3} = \frac{\partial x_2}{\partial p_3} + x_3 \frac{\partial x_2}{\partial M} = -\frac{M p_4 p_1}{(2p_1 p_2 + 2p_3 p_4)^2} < 0$$

and

$$\frac{\delta x_2}{\delta p_1} = \frac{\partial x_2}{\partial p_1} + x_1 \frac{\partial x_2}{\partial M} = \frac{2M p_3 p_4 + M p_1 p_2}{(2p_1 p_2 + 2p_3 p_4)^2} > 0$$

Similar relations hold for other pairs of goods. Furthermore, since,

$$\frac{\partial x_2}{\partial M} \frac{\partial x_3}{\partial M} = \frac{p_1 p_4}{(2p_1 p_2 + 2p_3 p_4)^2}$$

we have

$$\frac{\delta x_2}{\delta p_3} = \lambda \frac{\partial x_2}{\partial M} \frac{\partial x_3}{\partial M}$$

where $\lambda = (-m)$ and is, as required by our general theory, independent of the particular pair of goods taken one from each of the two different groups. We also deduce that within-groups pairs of goods are gross substitutes while between-groups pairs are gross complements. The economic intuition of this type of situation is that goods are naturally divided into groups such that within a group, each good is a rival for every other, while goods from different groups tend to go together in consumption. Thus the two groups might be food and drink with different varieties of food being substitutes for one another while any one type of food and any one type of drink tend to go together in consumption. A theoretical model similar in spirit to this has been formulated in [38, 27]. Here consumers' preferences are supposed to depend not on goods for their own sake but on the characteristics that goods possess. Thus various types of clothing may give satisfaction not in themselves at all, but indirectly through their warmth or their fashionability, so that clothing will enter the utility function only through a function which states the characteristics offered by clothing. Suppose that each good possesses only a single characteristic and that there are more goods available than characteristics. (Both these are very strong assumptions: a motor car would generally be thought of as a complicated package of qualities and not a single quality, while if each good is differentiated from every other in the eyes of the consumer then it seems likely that any particular good would possess the characteristic peculiar to itself of being itself). Then if $(x_1 \ldots x_n)$ are quantities of goods and $(z_1 \ldots z_m)$ are characteristics, we can write the utility function as

$$u = u(z_1(x_1 \ldots x_p)z_2(x_{p+1} \ldots x_q) \ldots z_m(x_s \ldots x_n)$$

where the goods are split into groups in such a way that any pair of goods within a group possess the same characteristic while pairs of goods from different groups possess distinct characteristics. Hence in this special case, Lancaster's approach [38] can be interpreted as an intuitive justification for a separable utility function; it defines the kinds of worlds in which one might expect these types of utility function to be important. However, goods may contribute towards more than a single characteristic and there may be some qualities which can be enjoyed only from the simultaneous consumption of several goods, so that there is a form of consumption externality in that the total of consumption of several goods yield a joint characteristic. It is also possible that in any situation there may be more characteristics than goods if, for example, these interaction phenomena are prevalent. In general then this yields a form of utility function

$$u = u\{z_1(\mathbf{x}_1, \mathbf{y}) \ldots z_m(\mathbf{x}_m, \mathbf{y}), z_{m+1}(\mathbf{y})\},$$

where $\mathbf{y}$ is some subset of the goods, which is a fairly natural generalisation of the separable functions. The approach can be developed a little to bring out some of the implicit economics: since consumers' preferences depend on the qualities that goods possess and not on the goods themselves, one might expect that in equilibrium positions, there will be 'shadow prices' of the characteristics reflecting the marginal valuations of consumers for each of the characteristics. To illustrate this possibility, suppose that the relation between characteristics and goods is linear; i.e. each characteristic z_i can be expressed as a linear combination, say $\Sigma b_{ij}x_j$, of the quantities of goods consumed so that we have $\mathbf{z} = B\mathbf{x}$ where B is a matrix of the $|b_{ij}|$ [8]. We may proceed as above, regarding the utility function as a function of the z_i and maximising it subject to a budget constraint expressed only in terms of the z_i. In order to do this we must find an equation which describes the same consumption possibilities as the equation $\sum_i p_i x_i = M$ but which involves the z_i and which has a natural interpretation in terms of the expenditure on the characteristics valued at the 'shadow prices' of the characteristics not exceeding income. Suppose we let $\mathbf{w}$ be a vector of shadow prices of the z_i, at present undefined. Then we would like to be able to write $\sum_i w_i z_i = M$ as the budget constraint. Since $\mathbf{z} = B\mathbf{x}$ and the actual behavioural constraint has the form $\sum_i p_i x_i = M$, a little reflection indicates that, on the assumption that B is non-singular, $\mathbf{w} = (B^{-1})'\mathbf{p}$ would be a suitable definition for $\mathbf{w}$ since

$$\sum_i w_i z_i = (\mathbf{w}', \mathbf{z}) = (\mathbf{p}'B^{-1}, B\mathbf{x}) = \sum_i p_i z_i = M$$

where $(\mathbf{w}', \mathbf{z})$ is shorthand notation for the operation of summing the cross products of terms in two vectors. Hence

$w_i = \sum_j B_{ij} p_j$, where B_{ij} are the relevant elements of the transposed inverse matrix of B, is the 'price' the consumer has to pay to purchase a unit of the ith characteristic through purchasing goods. As one would expect, it is a linear combination of the actual market prices of the goods that contribute towards the ith characteristic. The assumption that $z_i(\mathbf{x})$ can be expressed as $z_i = \sum_j b_{ij} x_j$ ensures that the b_{ij} are independent of the x's and so we can define prices for the z_i whether or not we are in equilibrium. In general the b_{ij} will reflect the indirect marginal utility of goods and may not be constant.

In summary, the material of this section concerns some additional restrictions which might be placed on the form of the utility function. Since there is an infinite variety of such restrictions that could be made, attention has concentrated either on those restrictions that formally express intuitive situations, such as that arising when substitute/complement relations between goods are discussed, or on restrictions that efficiently summarise the vast amount of information contained within a complete system of demand functions. If utility functions are separable then many substitution effects between pairs of goods from different groups need never be considered since these are known once the income terms for every good are known. We do, however, need to know a single between group substitution effect in the case of additively separable utility in order to be able to calculate the proportionality factor λ while with separable utility we need one between-group substitution term for every pair of groups r and s in order to be able to deduce the proportionality factors λ^{rs}. Nevertheless it appears that separable utility analyses have an intuitively satisfying content and go quite a long way towards summarising the information in a demand function system.

Note that any hypothesis about separable utility is of a compound nature involving both a hypothesis about the grouping of goods and a hypothesis about the form of interaction between groups. The hypothesis as to the grouping selected could be based on an *a priori* judgement but it would also be possible to conduct psychological surveys to attempt to discover the linking patterns between goods in consumers' minds.

THE THEORY OF HOMOTHETIC UTILITY FUNCTIONS

A further type of indifference map which is often found to be useful in economic work is the homothetic indifference map.

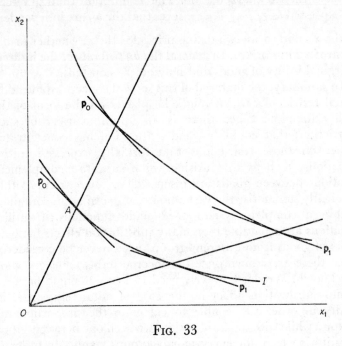

Fig. 33

An indifference map defined over n goods is said to be homothetic if the marginal rates of substitution between every pair of goods at any point $(x_1, \ldots x_n)$ is equal to that between the corresponding pair of goods at any other point $(y_1 \ldots y_n)$ in which the consumption of each good, y_i, is proportional to the consumption of each good in the original position, x_i. Thus in the simple two-dimensional case shown in Fig. 33, if we take any point such as A in the plane and calculate the marginal rate of substitution at that point, then at all points on the line through the origin and A, the marginal rate of substitution of the different indifference curves through these points must be equal to that at A. This condition must hold for any point like A and so it is fairly clear that if the indifference map is homothetic then if we know any one indifference curve then we know the whole indifference map. For example, if we are given the curve II, then we can construct all other indifference curves from it by taking all rays through the origin with their associated marginal rate of substitution found from the curve II and integrating these marginal rates of substitution to produce the other indifference curves.

Most of the market implications of a homothetic indifference map are immediately apparent. Since with this type of indifference map, one indifference curve is much the same as another then one would expect that the level of income does not alter the composition of consumer purchases. This is in fact clearly the case; consider an Engel curve for any fixed prices. Then we know that all points on a line through the origin with marginal rates of substitution given by the fixed price ratios all belong to the Engel curve. We also know that by non-satiation for any good, the Engel curve must always have a positive slope and that because indifference curves are strictly convex to the origin the marginal rate of substitution cannot be the same at two different points on the same indifference curve. Hence the only points which can belong to an Engel curve are those points on the particular straight line through the origin corresponding to the relevant marginal rates of substitution. Hence any given Engel curve being a straight line through the origin has a constant slope so that

$$\frac{\partial x_i / \partial M}{\partial x_j / \partial M} = k_{ij}$$

at all income levels for the given prices. However, k_{ij} measures the slope of a straight line through the origin; consequently any point (x_i, x_j) on this straight line satisfies the equation $x_i/x_j = k_{ij}$ and we have

$$\frac{\partial x_i / \partial M}{\partial x_j / \partial M} = \frac{x_i}{x_j}$$

If the indifference map is homothetic then all goods are purchased in fixed ratios as income varies with constant prices. An

D

equivalent way of stating this property is that a given percentage change in income with prices constant leads to an equal percentage change in the purchases of all goods, i.e. all income elasticities are equal. But we are assuming that all income is spent so that if income varies by 1 per cent then so does total expenditure. This means that since all income elasticities are equal, they must all be equal to unity. A further implication of a homothetic indifference map which occasionally proves useful is that in this case since

$$x_i \frac{\partial x_j}{\partial M} = x_j \frac{\partial x_i}{\partial M}$$

the total effects of a price change

$$\frac{\partial x_i}{\partial p_j} = \frac{\delta x_i}{\delta p_j} - x_j \frac{\partial x_i}{\partial M}$$

are symmetric so that $\partial x_i / \partial p_j = \partial x_j / \partial p_i$. Hence in this case it is true that if good i is a gross complement for good j then good j must also be a gross complement for good i.

One example of a homothetic indifference map, which also happens to be separable, is that already given of

$$u(x_1, \ldots x_n) = \phi \left(\sum_{i=1}^{n} a_i \log x_i \right)$$

where the demand functions had the form

$$x_i = \frac{a_i}{\sum_{j=1}^{n} a_j} \frac{M}{p_i}$$

The marginal rate of substitution between goods i and j is $a_i x_j / a_j x_i$ which will be constant if both x_i and x_j are varied in the same proportion. Similarly from the demand functions, the income elasticity is

$$\frac{M}{x_i} \frac{\partial x_i}{\partial M} = \frac{M}{a_i M} p_i \sum_{u=1}^{n} a_j \frac{a_i}{p_i \sum_{i=1}^{n} a_j} = 1$$

Moreover the total price effects are certainly symmetric, $\partial x_i / \partial p_j = \partial x_j / \partial p_i$, since each of these expressions is identically zero.

The Stone linear expenditure system proper generalises this example by changing the point from which the indifference map is homothetic away from the origin and to any other point. Thus if the utility function can be written:

$$u(x_1 \ldots x_n) = \sum_{i=1}^{n} a_i \log(x_i - b_i)$$

then the demand functions are said to satisfy Stones linear expenditure system. Here the marginal rate of substitution between goods i and j,

$$\frac{a_i(x_j - b_j)}{a_j(x_i - b_i)}$$

is not necessarily constant if goods i and j undergo proportional quantity variations. However, if the 'goods quantities' $(x_i - b_i)$

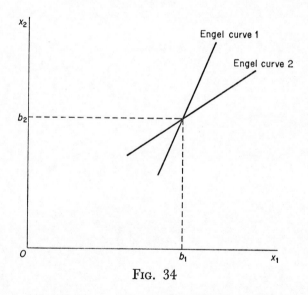

FIG. 34

and $(x_j - b_j)$ undergo proportional changes, then the marginal rate of substitution is constant. The situation can be represented diagrammatically as shown in Fig. 34; there are still linear Engel curves for each good but instead of coming from the origin these Engel curves come from the point $(b_1 \ldots b_n)$.

The interested reader should be able easily to calculate the restrictions on the demand functions coming from this system of preferences. Economically the hypothesis that the indifference map be of the Stone form is more acceptable than that it should be homothetic from the origin. In the latter case, no luxuries or necessities are possible at all; at all income levels there has to be a proportionate allocation of income to goods. In the Stone system, however, there has only to be a proportionate allocation between goods of the part of income which remains after the 'essential' quantities b_i of each good i have been purchased.

5 Extensions and Limitations

The vast body of accepted demand theory outlined in the preceding pages proceeds from some basic postulates as to how consumers behave in order to deduce implications about their behaviour. The purpose of all this is at least twofold: first, if the fundamental postulates of consumer behaviour appear to be reasonable, then we have learnt something about the way in which the demand forces in the economy actually work; second, if we have a reasonable representation of how demand influences the functioning of the system then we might be able to control and regulate the economy or sectors of the economy. For example, if we are confident in our model, then we should be able to advise governments and other organisations as to the likely effects of a particular purchase tax policy or a particular pricing policy by firms. If the government levies a purchase tax on a good, keeping all other things constant, then, since $\delta x_i / \delta p_i \leqslant 0$, we could predict that purchases of the good would fall so long as the good was not inferior. We must then assess the extent to which our theory can cope with the twin requirements of explanation and prediction.

Consider the first requirement: in some respects it could be argued that the body of theory is an inaccurate representation of reality, while in other respects it is incomplete. In reality, consuming units consist of families the members of which interact with one another. As such the family does not appear to possess a well-defined preference ordering; each family member has his own preference ordering and the total of family income is allocated to satisfy the desires of each family member generally in a way determined by the family autocrat. It may well be that when family income is high, a higher proportion of income is devoted to the minority members of the family than when family income is low. If we then try to combine the dif-

ferent preference orderings of the different family members to
deduce an overall family ordering which can be maximised
subject to a budget constraint then the relative importance of
the different individual orderings within the total will depend
on the level of family income. Hence the overall family preference ordering is not defined independently of the budgetary
situation which the family faces: prices and/or income would
enter the family utility function. One way of overcoming this
difficulty would be to adopt Friedman's permanent income
hypothesis: the utility maximisation hypothesis applies to
average budgetary situations giving us an average or 'usual
family' utility function, but in any particular situation there
may be deviations from this average [23, 24].

The conventional theory requires that each consumer should
be capable of ordering in a transitive fashion every pair of
commodity bundles which he could conceivably obtain.
However, consumers might well be unable to order precisely
bundles of widely different composition consisting largely of
goods outside their realm of experience, because of their
ignorance of the nature of the goods involved. Similarly, due
to the consumer's imperfect knowledge of the precise structure
of his own tastes, he might find it very difficult to order with
certainty commodity bundles that are very close together in
their composition. For example, the ordering of the two
bundles:

$$A = (4 \text{ oz fish}; 6 \text{ oz chips})$$
$$B = (4\tfrac{1}{2} \text{ oz fish}; 5 \text{ oz chips})$$

might be expected to present difficulties. There are several
ways in which we can seek to represent this behaviour in a
model. We could attempt to construct a theory which allows
for some degree of non-comparability of bundles [4, 5, 6]. Or
we could recognise that all bundles are comparable but that
while strict preference is transitive indifference is intransitive
[2, 3, 32, 34]. Finally, we could attempt to take account of
the randomness implicit in choice behaviour due to the various
types of ignorance of the consumer [11]. The first approach
entails the definition of a utility function over the commodity
space which will truly reflect the ordering of pairs of bundles

which are comparable: thus if xPy then $u(x) > u(y)$ and if xIy then $u(x) = u(y)$ although we cannot deduce from knowledge of $u(x)$ and $u(y)$ alone whether x and y are comparable.

In order for the utility function to adequately represent market choices it is necessary that there should exist some utility function which, when maximised over the feasible bundles available as given for example by a budget constraint, should select all bundles which are maximal in the sense of the ordering

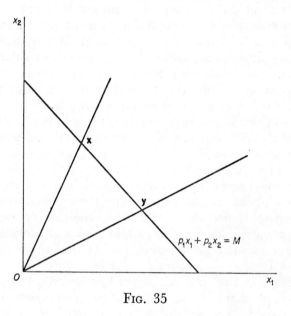

FIG. 35

out of all feasible bundles. For example, suppose that in the plane, a preference relation satisfies the condition that any bundles lying on the same line through the origin are comparable with bundles being preferred the further they are from the origin but that bundles which are not proportional are not comparable. We then require that the utility function when maximised subject to a budget constraint should pick out all bundles such as **x** and **y** lying along the budget line (Fig. 35), each of which is no lower in the ordering than any other feasible bundle. With this ordering any linear function $c_1 x_1 + c_2 x_2 (c_1, c_2 > 0)$ will represent the ordering in the sense that xPy implies $c_1 x_1 + c_2 x_2 > c_1 y_1 + c_2 y_2$ but any particular linear function with particular values of c_1 and c_2 will establish a utility ordering between non-comparable bundles which may well be irrelevant to the consumers preference ordering. If this particular utility function is selected and maximised subject to a budget constraint, then one or more of a wider range of non-comparable maximal bundles will be selected, although in this budgetary situation the consumer may actually have chosen one of the different non-comparable bundles. Hence some interest attaches to ensuring that all non-comparable bundles which could each be maximal in any particular budgetary situation are assigned the same values by the utility function. Note that even if we could lay down sufficient restrictions on the preference ordering to ensure that an appropriate utility function representing it was continuous, there would still be difficulties in applying the standard analysis of demand theory, since instead of a single bundle being selected in each price/income situation a whole range of non-comparable maximal bundles would be selected.

This may seem a somewhat unsatisfactory conclusion: although choice is determinate our theory does not yield determinate choice, but in the non-comparable case just selects a variety of non-comparable maximal bundles. The consumer presumably has some rule of thumb for choosing between these non-comparable bundles; if we tried to take account of this then it may well not be transitive. Basically we only get out what is put in: if we postulate consumer ignorance then it should not be surprising that we conclude that consumers do not make determinate choices.

It is fairly easy to see that this approach is quite general; many different degrees of non-comparability can be accommodated so long as the comparable bundles are ordered in a way which allows representation by a utility function (i.e. in particular in a transitive fashion) and so long as the actual ordering can be extended over the non-comparable bundles to define a fictitious ordering which satisfies continuity and transitivity conditions. At a formal level the main problem in developing the theory is to ensure that the restrictions laid down in the partial preference ordering to ensure sufficient continuity of some fictitious ordering over the whole space are not so strong as to severely limit the type of non-comparability possible. For example, Schmeidler [54] has demonstrated that if there is a transitive preference relation which satisfies some rather stringent continuity conditions then in fact this preference relation can admit no non-comparabilities at all. In this connection the precise formulation of the axioms becomes rather important; for example, if we wish to capture the essence of

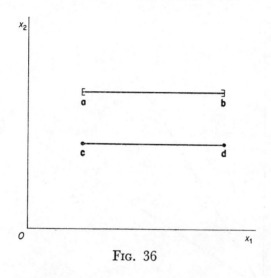

FIG. 36

non-comparability then instead of requiring the preference relation to be transitive it may be more natural to require it to be what might be termed comparably-transitive: i.e. if xPy and yPx and x and z are comparable, then xPz.

Intuitively the continuity problem arises because with non-comparability of some pairs of bundles the gaps between bundles in the ordering may be much larger than the physical distance between bundles. Let the space be the plane and suppose that in the plane all comparable bundles lie in two intervals, $[\mathbf{a}, \mathbf{b}]$ and $[\mathbf{c}, \mathbf{d}]$ (Fig. 36). The points $\mathbf{b}, \mathbf{c}, \mathbf{d}$ are not comparable with any other point but $\mathbf{a}$ is comparable with all points in the interior of the two intervals. The ordering is such that any point in the interior of the interval $[a, b]$ is at least as desired as any point in the interior of the interval $[c, d]$ but every point in the interior of either interval is strictly preferred to **a**. If we then take a sequence $\{\mathbf{x}_i\}$ of bundles belonging only to the interior of $[a, b]$ and converging to **a** and any fixed bundle **y** in the interior of $[c, d]$ then if a continuous utility function were to exist we would require $u(\mathbf{x}_i) > u(\mathbf{y}) \Rightarrow \lim_{i \to \infty} \{u(\mathbf{x}_i)\} = u(\mathbf{a}) \geqslant u(\mathbf{y})$ which cannot hold for any function representing the ordering. Hence in this case

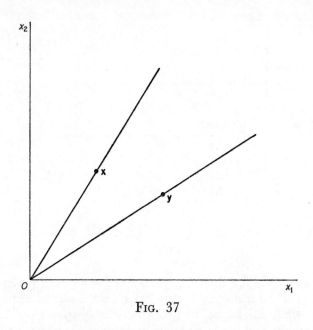

Fig. 37

no utility function exists. Note that the problem arises because **a** lies much further from points of $[a, b]$ in the ordering sense than in the physical sense. A second example again concerns the plane [47]; the ordering is such that $\mathbf{x}P\mathbf{y}$ if and only if $x_1 y_2 > x_2 y_1$ (Fig. 37). Hence all points on any ray through the origin are non-comparable; points along the vertical axis are superior to all points along any other ray through the origin and points along the horizontal axis are inferior to points on any other ray. Furthermore points on steeper rays such as **x** are superior to points on flatter rays such as **y**. If we define a utility function

$$u(x_1, x_2) = \frac{x_1}{x_2} x_2 > 0$$

then because of

$$u(x_1, 0) = \infty \qquad u(0, x_2) = 0$$

i.e. the large difference in utility values of points which are close together but one of which is on the vertical and the other on the horizontal axis, it is impossible to choose a utility value for the origin $u(0, 0)$ so as to make the utility function continuous.

Finally, of course, in the non-comparable case, if we wish to preserve particular properties of the utility function such as a diminishing marginal rate of substitution or non-satiation, then we have to impose still stronger requirements on the way in which non-comparability arises [6].

We shall briefly mention the approach of assuming indifference to be intransitive primarily as an introduction to the third approach. Assume that there exists a continuous utility function over the commodity space which represents a complete preference ordering in which strict preference is transitive but any two commodity bundles **x**, **y** such that $|u(\mathbf{x}) - u(\mathbf{y})| > a$ are indifferent. Here a is any number generally thought of as being 'small'; one interpretation [22, 3] of this situation is that, due to imperfections in the powers of discrimination of the consumer between the 'utility-value' of pairs of bundles, the consumer is incapable of ranking in a strict order bundles which have a small but non-zero utility difference. Note that this implies a cardinal measure of utility since we may have

$$|u(\mathbf{x}) - u(\mathbf{y})| < a \quad \text{but} \quad |\phi\{u(\mathbf{x})\} - \phi\{u(\mathbf{y})\}| > a$$

where $\phi(.)$ is a general monotonic function of one variable. We may change the origin of the utility function and if we are prepared to let a depend on the scale of the utility function then we can change this scale, so that

$$|u(\mathbf{x}) - u(\mathbf{y})| < a \quad \text{if and only if}$$
$$|\{a + bu(\mathbf{x})\} - \{a + bu(\mathbf{y})\}| < \beta$$

We may replace the utility function $u(x)$ only by utility functions of the form $w(\mathbf{x}) = a + bu(\mathbf{x})$ and in this sense we require cardinality. If we now face the consumer with a budget constraint and seek to find the demand functions, then any bundle $\mathbf{x}$ which can be purchased, given the price and income situation, and which has utility $u(\mathbf{x})$ no more than a units below the utility of any other bundle $\mathbf{y}$ which satisfies the budget constraint, may be selected by the consumer who maximises his utility within the limits of his perception. Since there may be many such bundles, the demand functions will not in general be single-valued but will assign a range of bundles which are maximising to a particular choice situation. Furthermore it is possible that one maximising bundle may have a little more of one good and no less of any other than another maximising bundle. Hence it will not always be true that all income is spent. There appear to remain several unanswered questions with this approach. First, where does the postulated 'true' utility function come from and how can we attempt to test the theory to ensure it exists? Second, the imperfect discrimination leads to bands of bundles close together between which the consumer is ignorant as to his true tastes: i.e. the consumer has no yardstick for evaluating the worth of these bundles. This is not the same thing, without an additional assumption of the rule of thumb the consumer adopts to choose between these bundles, as stating that the consumer is indifferent between them. Third, it does not necessarily seem reasonable that the limits of perception should depend only on utility differences between bundles rather than on the composition of the bundles themselves. For example, a consumer may always prefer one bundle to another if the former contains a small amount more of one good and no less of any other good compared to the latter.

In fact, some of these disadvantages are eliminated and the notion of imperfect discrimination and intransitive indifference may be presented as special cases, if we represent choice and preference in a probabilistic fashion [2, 11, 12, 40]. In an ordinal sense preference is nothing more or less than a statement by the consumer of which of two bundles he will choose in a given situation. This choice may in fact be random, either because the individual is uncertain as to the precise nature of the goods involved in the bundles, or as to the structure of his own tastes – i.e. the value of the perfectly perceived bundles to him. This leads us to suspect that a fairly accurate representation of choices might be to postulate that in any given situation, faced with choosing between two alternatives $\mathbf{x}$, $\mathbf{y}$, there is a certain probability $p(\mathbf{y}, \mathbf{x})$ that $\mathbf{y}$ will be chosen rather than $\mathbf{x}$ where $p(\mathbf{x}, \mathbf{y}) + p(\mathbf{y}, \mathbf{x}) = 1$, $1 \geqslant p(\mathbf{x}, \mathbf{y}) \geqslant 0$. This model might also be taken as an explanation of the apparent inconsistency of choices revealed by individuals choosing differently between $\mathbf{x}$, $\mathbf{y}$ on successive occasions in similar situations. Indifference and preference as such do not exist, but we may identify particular values of the probabilities with those limits of choice. Thus $p(\mathbf{x}, \mathbf{y}) = 1$ is often taken as meaning $\mathbf{x}$ is preferred to $\mathbf{y}$ and $p(\mathbf{x}, \mathbf{y}) = \frac{1}{2}$ as $\mathbf{x}$ is indifferent to $\mathbf{y}$. We may also impose transitivity conditions on the probabilities without actually requiring transitivity of indifference or strict preference. Thus we may require

$$p(\mathbf{x}, \mathbf{y}) \geqslant p(\mathbf{y}, \mathbf{x}) \text{ and } p(\mathbf{y}, \mathbf{z}) \geqslant p(\mathbf{z}, \mathbf{y}) \Rightarrow p(\mathbf{x}, \mathbf{z}) \geqslant p(\mathbf{z}, \mathbf{x}) \text{ for all } \mathbf{x}, \mathbf{y}, \mathbf{z}$$

without requiring transitive indifference or strict preference. If we have only a finite collection of bundles to order, then, given that a probability exists for every pair of alternatives, and given the transitivity condition, we may rank the bundles according to the probability with which each is selected over every other bundle in a consistent fashion. We can arrange the bundles $(\mathbf{x}_1, \ldots, \mathbf{x}_n)$ so that

$$p(\mathbf{x}_1, \mathbf{x}_2) \geqslant p(\mathbf{x}_2, \mathbf{x}_1)$$
$$p(\mathbf{x}_2, \mathbf{x}_3) \geqslant p(\mathbf{x}_3, \mathbf{x}_2), \ldots, p(\mathbf{x}_{n-1}, \mathbf{x}_n) \geqslant p(\mathbf{x}_{n, n-1})$$

and by transitivity

$$p(\mathbf{x}_1, \mathbf{x}_i) \geqslant p(\mathbf{x}_i, \mathbf{x}_1) \quad (i = 2, \ldots, n)$$
$$p(\mathbf{x}_2, \mathbf{x}_i) \geqslant p(\mathbf{x}_i, \mathbf{x}_2) \quad (i = 3, \ldots, n, \text{etc.})$$

and then assign utilities n to $\mathbf{x}_1$, $(n-1)$ to $\mathbf{x}, \ldots, 0$ to $\mathbf{x}_n$ and have an integer-valued utility function such that

$$u(\mathbf{x}_i) \geqslant u(\mathbf{x}_j) \quad \text{if and only if} \quad p(\mathbf{x}_i, \mathbf{x}_j) \geqslant p(\mathbf{x}_j, \mathbf{x}_i)$$

Note that any monotonic increasing transformation of this utility function will also suffice as a utility function. If we then maximise this utility function subject to a budget constraint and derive the demand functions, then these demand functions will show for each price and income situation the bundle which the consumer will be most likely to choose in that situation.

We may also proceed to lay down stronger additional conditions to be satisfied by the probabilities $p(\mathbf{x}, \mathbf{y})$ and explore the implications of these conditions for the form of the function representing the preference ordering. Thus Debreu [16] has shown that if for all combinations of four alternatives $(\mathbf{x}, \mathbf{y}, \mathbf{w}, \mathbf{z})$ it is true that the axiom

$$p(\mathbf{x}, \mathbf{y}) \leqslant p(\mathbf{w}, \mathbf{z}) \quad \text{if and only if} \quad p(\mathbf{x}, \mathbf{w}) \leqslant p(\mathbf{y}, \mathbf{z})$$

and a rather strong continuity axiom holds, then there exists a utility function $u(\mathbf{x})$ such that

$$p(\mathbf{x}, \mathbf{y}) \leqslant p(\mathbf{w}, \mathbf{z}) \quad \text{if and only if} \quad u(\mathbf{x}) - u(\mathbf{y}) \leqslant u(\mathbf{w}) - u(\mathbf{z})$$

If we interpret $p(\mathbf{x}, \mathbf{y})$ as meaning the degree of preference of $\mathbf{x}$ over $\mathbf{y}$, then the theorem states that there exists a utility function unique up to a transformation of the form $au(\mathbf{x}) + b$ in which degrees of preference are preserved and measured by utility differences. The axiom represents a form of independence condition: degrees of preference in one situation should be carried over into other situations. If we know $p(\mathbf{x}, \mathbf{y}) \leqslant p(\mathbf{w}, \mathbf{z})$ and know the value of $p(\mathbf{y}, \mathbf{z})$ then we have an upper limit for the possible value of $p(\mathbf{x}, \mathbf{w})$. Since it is conceivable to test this axiom experimentally by observing an individual's choices between alternatives a large number of times, and hence to estimate the probabilities, we have a test of whether individual behaviour can be represented by a cardinal utility function.

The probabilistic approach can be extended by assuming that we can represent consumer behaviour by a model of the following kind. Given a finite collection of possible commodity bundles $(\mathbf{x}_1 \ldots \mathbf{x}_n)$, there exists a probability distribution defined over all logically possible rankings of the bundles. Thus any ranking corresponds to an arrangement of the n bundles in a particular order (e.g. with three bundles, say,

$\mathbf{x}_2, \mathbf{x}_1, \mathbf{x}_3$) where the first bundle is the first in the ranking; the second is the second in the ranking and so on. For each such possible ranking r, there exists a probability $p(r)$ that this is the actual ranking used by the consumer in any situation. Furthermore the sum of these probabilities over all possible rankings is unity. This is perhaps the case in which the uncertainty of choice is most closely related to the consumer's uncertainty of his tastes; once the ranking is given, then choice is determinate, but since the ranking itself is random, choice is random. In [12] Block and Marschak link together the uncertainty of choice and of the relevant ranking in a more direct fashion. Let M represent any subcollection of all commodity bundles, e.g. $M = (\mathbf{x}_1, \dots, \mathbf{x}_m)$ and let $p(\mathbf{x}_i; M)$ represent the probability of choosing the bundle $\mathbf{x}_i$ when the consumer is offered all the bundles in M as alternatives. Finally, let R_{im} consist of all those rankings of the commodity bundles in M (ignoring the ranking of bundles outside M) in which $\mathbf{x}_i$ is the first or top bundle. Then, if $p(\mathbf{x}_i; M) = \sum_{r \text{ in } R_{im}} p(r)$ it can be shown that the probability distribution of rankings can be represented by a utility function in the following sense. There exists a random function $u(\mathbf{x})$ defined at $\mathbf{x}_1, \dots, \mathbf{x}_n$ and unique up to a monotonic transformation such that for any bundle $\mathbf{x}_i$ in any subcollection of bundles M of $(\mathbf{x}_1, \dots, \mathbf{x}_n)$

$$p(\mathbf{x}_i; M) = \text{probability } \{u(\mathbf{x}_i) > u(\mathbf{x}_j) \text{ all } \mathbf{x}_j \text{ in } M\}.$$

Thus if the actual choice probability can be written as the sum of the probabilities of those rankings occurring in which $\mathbf{x}_i$ is ranked top, then the actual choice probability can also be expressed as the probability of the random utility of $\mathbf{x}_i$ exceeding that of all other bundles $\mathbf{x}_j$. Note that if we actually have a random utility distribution with the necessary link between observed choice probabilities and the randomness of tastes, then we should also expect to be able to interpret Debreu's utility differences result in terms of an underlying random utility function, given some additional conditions on decomposing $p(\mathbf{x}_i; M)$ and hence $p(r)$ into the choice probabilities for pairwise choices $p(\mathbf{x}_i, \mathbf{x}_j)$. What implications has this for market analysis? Suppose that we postulate the existence of a random utility function $u(\mathbf{x})$ specifying the way in which randomness enters. Then if we maximise the utility function subject to a budget constraint we deduce

$$\frac{\partial u(x)}{\partial x_i} = \lambda p_i \qquad \sum p_i x_i = M$$

where in general $\partial u / \partial x_i$ and λ are random. If we solve these equations for the $\mathbf{x}$ and λ as functions of (p, m), then each x_i will be a random function of prices and income. Thus, instead of a single demand function, there will, for each good, be a whole probability distribution of demand functions. This is in fact what one would expect: if scatter diagrams of quantities, prices and income are observed from market data, typically the observations lie around a line rather than on a line. There are many different ways in which randomness might be introduced, but one rather attractive model might be to assume that the utility function could be written as $u(\mathbf{x}) = \phi\{\Sigma\, p_r v^r\,(\mathbf{x}_r, \epsilon_r)\}$ where $\mathbf{x}_r$ are subgroups of goods in the commodity bundle $\mathbf{x}$ and (p_r, ϵ_r) are each random variables for each r. p_r reflects the uncertainty of the consumer over the way in which different possible types of satisfaction are aggregated to yield overall utility. ϵ_r reflects uncertainty as to the production of these specific sources of satisfaction from the goods. Before leaving the topic, it should be mentioned that the randomness in choice is essentially due to uncertainty and ignorance. Hence, over time, or in repeated experiment, one might expect the consumer to learn gradually of the nature of the goods and of the structure of his tastes so that eventually choice might become completely determinate.

A further direction in which it might be felt that the conventional theory is an inaccurate representation for at least some goods concerns the possibility that preferences should depend upon the budgetary situation faced [35]. It is often argued that for luxury goods such perhaps as jewellery or vintage wine, and also for complicated technical goods such as radios, the quality of a good may tend to be judged by its price. In other words the marginal utility of a good may depend not only on the quantities of all goods consumed but also on their price. If we are prepared to assume that the preference ordering changes in a smooth continuous fashion as the market prices vary, then we may represent the hypothesis by expressing the utility function as $u = u(\mathbf{x}, \mathbf{p})$ where $\mathbf{x}$ is the commodity bundle vector and $\mathbf{p}$ is the list of prices ruling. We could adopt more stringent hypotheses: for example, the judgement that quality tends to be assessed by price would be consistent with the view that only a relative price change affects the preference

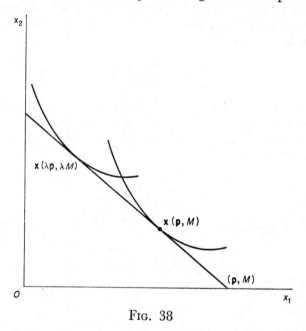

FIG. 38

ordering while a proportional change in all prices leaves the ranking of goods unchanged. This might lead to asserting that $u(\mathbf{x}, \mathbf{p}) = u(\mathbf{x}, \lambda\mathbf{p})$ for all positive numbers λ.

The major effects of assuming that the utility function depends in a general way on prices are twofold. First, if all prices and incomes change proportionally, then, although the bundles which may just be purchased remain unchanged, the relevant indifference map changes and hence the optimal quantities of goods may change (Fig. 38). This means that the demand functions $x_i = x_i(p, m)$ in general will not satisfy the property that $x_i(p, m) = x_i(\lambda p, \lambda m)$. There is some aspect of money illusion. Second, the composition of the substitution effect is different. Suppose the jth price changes and we wish to calculate the effect on purchases of x_i then the price change $\mathrm{d}p_j$ shifts the indifference map by $(\partial u/\partial p_j)\,\mathrm{d}p_j$: if $\partial u/\partial p_j > 0$ then on this account a cut in income is required when $\mathrm{d}p_j > 0$ to leave the consumer at the same utility level. On the other hand the cost of purchasing the originally chosen quantity x_j has changed by $x_j\,\mathrm{d}p_j$ and as in the traditional case compensation must be made for this. Hence the overall compensating income change is

$$\left\{ x_j - \frac{\partial u}{(\partial p_j/\lambda)} \right\} \mathrm{d}p_j$$

where we have divided $(\partial u/\partial p_j)\,\mathrm{d}p_j$ by the marginal utility of income to express the utility gain from the shift in the indifference map in money terms. Of this income change the consumer will spend

$$\left\{ x_j - \frac{\partial u}{(\partial p_j/\lambda)} \right\} \mathrm{d}p_j\, \frac{\partial x_i}{\partial m}$$

on the ith good. Hence the substitution effect can be written as

$$\frac{\partial x_i}{\partial p_j} = \frac{\partial x_i}{\partial p_j} + \left\{ x_j - \frac{\partial u}{(\partial p_j/\lambda)} \right\} \frac{\partial x_i}{\partial m}$$

It is also fairly clear that since price changes from different goods may shift the indifference map in different ways for different goods, then, in general, the substitution effects will no longer be symmetric. It can also be shown that in the absence of further specification of the way in which prices enter the utility function we lose the knowledge of signs of the substitution effects [35].

We now pass on to various respects in which the system of demand might be said to be incomplete. We first deal in a cursory way with the problems of interdependence, both in the sense of interdependence between consumers and in the sense of the way in which demand theory might interact with other theories in an overall explanation of the working of the economy. It appears likely that consumers, in their decision making, take account of the existence and behaviour of other consumers. First, if any consumer's utility function has the form $u = u(\mathbf{x}, M_B)$ where M_B represents the income of some other consumer so that in fact people are not insensitive to the income distribution, then it is open to any consumer to devote a part of his income to making a gift to other consumers. This can easily be incorporated into the conventional demand theory defining an additional good: 'money gifts to others' whose price is always unity and maximising,

$$u = u(x_1 \ldots x_n, x_{n+1})$$

subject to

$$\sum_{i=1}^{n} p_i x_i + x_{n+1} < M$$

Note that at maximising points the consumer will equate his marginal utility of income to his marginal utility of others' income.

In a similar fashion, but designed to describe Veblenesque effects, Duesenberry [20] postulated that the indifference map depends on the individual consumer's own position in the income distribution. In any given situation there will still be a determinate utility function and hence determinate demands for goods. However, if the income distribution changes, then the demand functions shift. Since some of the utility maximising choices consumers make concern their optimal supply of labour and hence their money income at the going wage, then there is an interdependence between tastes and the income distribution. The existing income distribution sets tastes and the supply of labour, and so the money income of each consumer. However, the money income of each consumer constitutes the income distribution. Depending on the way in which the supply of labour is determined by tastes, there may be a stable income distribution. Given this income distribution, utility maximising consumers each wish to supply just that amount of labour which will preserve the existing income distribution. Moreover any movements away from this distribution, due for example to money wage changes, may change tastes in such a way that the supply of labour adjusts so as to restore the previous income distribution. There is of course no guarantee that either of these possibilities occur.

Similar arguments apply to the more general case of externalities where each man's own preference ordering of his own consumption depends on the consumption of each good by each other consumer [30, 42]. Here, for fixed consumption patterns of all other customers, any particular consumer has a determinate preference ordering and hence determinate demand functions of the form $x_{ij} = f^{ij}$ ($\mathbf{p}$, M, $\mathbf{x}_k$) for consumption of the ith good by the jth consumer where $\mathbf{x}_k$ consists of the commodity bundle purchased by each other consumer k. In this case it can be shown that, under reasonable conditions, equilibrium commodity bundles demanded by each consumer do exist.

The conventional theory may also be said to be incomplete on the grounds that it is static: given the data that exists at a particular instant of time, then at that instant of time static demand functions with particular properties exist. However, as time passes, the data of the problem change. Tastes may change, due perhaps to advertising; the nature of goods may change and sometimes new goods may appear which did not previously exist. A complete theory of demand might be expected to have something to say about each of these phenomena. In a purely formal fashion, taste change may be represented parametrically by allowing the utility function to depend upon time [48]. For an explanation with a little more substance one might make the utility function depend parametrically on the past experience of the consumer, represented by a list of the totals of past consumption of each of the goods, in an attempt to explain the taste change as part of a learning process by the individual: from an initial approximate knowledge of his tastes, as his experience of a variety of consumption patterns grows, his knowledge of his 'true' tastes becomes increasingly precise. A more adequate explanation would explicitly introduce all the variables which might be expected to play a significant role in preference changes. Thus advertising and the degree of social contact with other consumers could both be included in an explicit model. Many formalisations of these notions are no doubt possible. The sort of model envisaged might take the following form: each consumer i has a utility function which is a function of his own consumption and total advertising expenditure in the economy $A(t)$ at a given time: $u_i = u_i \{\mathbf{x}_i, A(t)\}$. Moreover each consumer's marginal rates of substitution between goods changes in a way depending on the tastes of others and the degree of contact he has with others. For example, we might postulate that

$$\frac{\mathrm{d}}{\mathrm{d}t} \left\{ \frac{\partial u_i(\mathbf{x})/\partial x_r}{\partial u_i(\mathbf{x})/\partial x_s} \right\} = \alpha_i \left[\sum_{j=1}^{M} p_{ij} \left\{ \frac{\partial u_j(\mathbf{x})/\partial x_r}{\partial u_j(\mathbf{x})/\partial x_s} \right\} - \frac{\partial u_i(\mathbf{x})/\partial x_r}{\partial u_i(\mathbf{x})/\partial x_s} \right]$$

Where $p_{ij} = p_{ji}$ measures the degree of contact between individuals i and j. For example, p_{ij} could be the proportion of the total contact i and j have with all other individuals which they have with each other and so $\sum_j p_{ij} = \sum_i p_{ji} = 1$.

Moreover one might relate the p_{ij} to such socio-economic variables as income class, residential pattern, occupation, etc. on the grounds that similar people tend to mix more with one another than dissimilar people. The α_i might be interpreted as the susceptibility of the ith individual to the opinions and values of other individuals. Given these hypotheses and a set of data of prices and income of each consumer through time, then at each instant of time we could calculate the demands for goods made by each utility maximising consumer. Note that since the changes in the marginal rates of substitution depend upon the points at which they are evaluated, the whole process will heavily depend upon the commodity bundles from which the whole process starts. As a descriptive theory, this is perhaps as it should be.

Quality change in the nature of the goods will only be briefly mentioned, since we can in fact deal with this in a reasonable way by adopting the characteristics of goods approach outlined in the section on separability [23]. Thus suppose we allow the matrix B in that section to have a time trend $B = B(t)$; then the efficiency units of goods and the shadow prices of the efficiency units will both change over time. Hence for the given utility function actual quantities of the changing quality goods will vary over time. Moreover since changes in the quality of the goods mainly occur from factors on the supply side rather than originating with the consumer the hypothesis $B = B(t)$ may be reasonable within a theory of demand.

We have seen that, in some respects, demand theory is incomplete, while in a few other respects, the accuracy of its representation of behaviour may be in doubt. It remains to examine briefly the quantitative estimates that have been made of systems of demand functions from observations of market behaviour in different price/income situations. Although a thorough understanding of econometric technique is necessary to read all the work that has been done, it is possible to convey the flavour of the results without this. The computational problems of estimating the very large number of partial derivatives $\partial x_i / \partial p_j$, $\partial x_i / \partial M$ in a complete system of demand functions are enormous. Hence most of the work that has been done has been on additively separable systems of varying kinds, since this minimises the number of coefficients of the form $\partial x_i / \partial p_j$ to be estimated. From studies such as [7, 9, 10, 13, 14, 15, 33, 39, 46, 50], several broad trends emerge. First, there is, in general, a prevalence of gross complementarity between goods: $\partial x_i / \partial p_j < 0$ despite the fact that in many cases the substitution effect alone is positive. Hence from the systems that have been estimated, income effects appear to be typically stronger than substitution effects. However, for almost all goods in all studies, $\partial x_i / \partial p_i < 0$ so that very few goods are sufficiently inferior for the positive income effect to outweigh the negative substitution effect. There is also a fairly strong tendency in all these studies for goods such as food to be income inelastic, but for goods such as consumer durables to be income elastic. This is exactly what we would expect, and what has long been enshrined in economics in the form of Engel's law. The only empirical work which actually sets out to test whether substitution effects are symmetric, demand functions homogeneous of degree zero, and the hypothesis that all income is spent, occurs in [31, 14]. The results indicate that, overall, most of the substitution effects were symmetric, but that in general the data did not support the hypothesis that the demand functions are homogeneous of degree zero; nor that the budget constraint always holds with equality. This might seem to indicate that money illusion and satiation with respect to some goods may be empirically important. Even without requiring homogeneity or equality in the budget constraint there was still a prevalence of gross complementarity relations between goods. Moreover in this same context, as one might expect, there appeared to be several fairly strongly inferior goods: several of the $\partial x_i / \partial p_i$ are positive. However, even these broad results are open to criticism quite apart from the precise numerical estimates, since so many strong assumptions have to be made in order to be able to apply the theory directly to the market observations.

References

[1] M. Allais, 'Le Comportement de l'homme rationnel devant le Risque', *Econometrica* (1953).

[2] W. Armstrong, 'The Determinateness of the Utility Function', *Economic Journal* (1939).

[3] W. Armstrong, 'A Note on the theory of Consumer Behaviour', *Oxford Economic Papers* (1950).

[4] R. Aumann, 'Utility Theory Without the Completeness Axiom', *Econometrica* (1962).

[5] R. Aumann, 'Utility Theory Without the Completeness Axiom: A Correction', *Econometrica* (1964).

[6] R. Aumann, 'Subjective Programming', in *Human Judgements and Optimality*, ed. M. Shelley and G. Bryan: (New York: Wiley, 1964).

[7] R. Ayanian, 'A Comparison of Barten's Estimated Demand Elasticities with those Obtained Using Frisch's Method', *Econometrica* (1969).

[8] A. P. Barten, 'Family Composition and Expenditure', in *Econometric Analysis for National Economic Planning*, ed. P. Hart et. al. (Butterworth, 1964).

[9] A. P. Barten, 'Consumer Demand Functions Under Conditions of Almost Additive Preferences', *Econometrica* (1964).

[10] A. P. Barten, 'Estimating Demand Functions', *Econometrica* (1968).

[11] G. Becker, M. H. De Groot and J. Marschak, 'Stochastic Models of Choice Behaviour', *Behavioural Science* (1963).

[12] H. Block and J. Marschak, 'Random Orderings and Stochastic Theories of Responses', in *Contributions to Probability and Statistics*, ed. I. Olkin et al. (Stanford: Stanford University Press, 1960).

[13] R. P. Byron, 'Restricted Aitken Estimation of Sets of Demand Relations', *Econometrica* (1970).

[14] R. P. Byron, 'A Simple Method for Estimating Demand Systems Under Separable Utility Assumptions', *Review of Economic Studies* (1970).

[15] R. H. Court, 'Utility Maximisation and the Demand for New Zealand Meat', *Econometrica* (1967).

[16] G. Debreu, 'Stochastic Choice and Cardinal Utility', *Econometrica* (1958).

[17] G. Debreu, *Theory of Value* (New York: Wiley, 1959).

[18] G. Debreu, 'Topological Methods in Cardinal Utility Theory', in *Mathematical Methods in the Social Sciences*, ed. K. Arrow, S. Karlin and P. Suppes (Stanford: Stanford University Press, 1960).

[19] G. Debreu, 'Representation of a Preference Ordering by a Numerical Function', in *Decision Processes*, ed. R. M. Thrall, C. H. Coombs and R. L. Davies (New York: Wiley, 1954).

[20] J. Duesenberry, *Income, Saving and the Theory of Consumer Behaviour* (Cambridge, Mass.: Harvard University Press, 1949).

[21] W. Edwards, 'Theory of Decision Making'. *Psychological Bulletin*, 1954. Reprinted in *Decision Making*, ed. W. Edwards (Penguin, 1967).

[22] P. Fishburn, *Utility Theory for Decision Making* (New York: Wiley, 1970)

[23] F. Fisher and K. Shell, 'Taste and Quality Change', in *Value, Capital and Growth: Essays in honour of J. R. Hicks*, ed. J. Wolfe (Edinburgh University Press, 1968).

[24] M. Friedman, *Theory of the Consumption Function* (Princeton, N.J.: Princeton University Press, 1957).

[25] N. Georgescu-Roegen, *Analytical Economics* (Cambridge Mass.: Harvard University Press, 1966).

[26] W. Gorman, 'Separable Utility and Aggregation', *Econometrica* (1958).

[27] W. Gorman, 'The Demand for Fish', report in *Econo-merica* (1960).

[28] W. Gorman, 'The Aggregation of Fixed Factors', in *Value, Capital and Growth*, ed. J. Wolfe (Edinburgh University Press, 1968).

[29] W. Gorman, 'The Structure of Utility Functions', *Review of Economic Studies* (1968).

*[30] H. A. J. Green, *Consumer Theory* (Penguin, 1971).

[31] J. Hicks, *Value and Capital* (Oxford University Press, 1946).

[32] H. Houthakker, 'Revealed Preference and the Utility Function', *Economica* (1950).

*[33] H. Houthakker, 'Additive Preferences', *Econometrica* (1960).

[34] D. Jamison and L. Lau, 'Semiorders, Revealed Preference and the Theory of Consumer Demand', Technical Report No. 31 (Institute for Mathematical Studies in the Social Sciences, Stanford University).

[35] P. Kalman, 'Theory of Consumer Behaviour when Prices Enter the Utility Function', *Econometrica* (1968).

[36] S. Karlin, *Mathematical Methods in Games, Programming and Economics*, vol. I, Appendix B (Reading, Mass.: Addison Wesley, 1959).

[37] D. Katzner, *Static Demand Theory* (Collier Macmillan, 1970).

[38] K. Lancaster, 'A New Approach to Consumer Theory', *Journal of Political Economy* (1966).

[39] C. Leser, 'Commodity Group Expenditure Functions for the UK', *Econometrica* (1961).

[40] R. D. Luce, *Individual Choice Behaviour* (New York: Wiley, 1959).

[41] K. May, 'Transitivity, Utility and Aggregation in Preference Theory', *Econometrica* (1954).

[42] L. McKenzie, 'Competitive Equilibrium with Dependent Consumer Preferences', in *2nd Symposium on Linear Programming* (National Bureau of Standards, Washington D.C., 1955).

[43] L. McKenzie, 'Demand Theory Without a Utility Index', *Review of Economic Studies* (1956–7).

[44] J. Meade, 'External Economies and Diseconomies in a Competitive Situation', *Economic Journal* (1952).

*[45] P. Newman, *The Theory of Exchange* (Englewood Cliffs, N.J.: Prentice-Hall, 1965).

[46] I. F. Pearce, *A Contribution to Demand Analysis* (Oxford University Press, 1964).

[47] B. Peleg, 'Utility Functions for Partially Ordered Topological Spaces', *Econometrica* (1970).

[48] M. Peston, 'Changing Utility Functions', in *Essays in Mathematical Economics in Honour of Oskar Morgenstern*, ed. M. Shubik (Princeton, N.J.: Princeton University Press).

[49] R. Pollak, 'The Implications of Separability', Discussion Paper (Department of Economics, University of Pennsylvania, 1966).

[50] A. Powell, 'A Complete System of Consumer Demand Equations for the Australian Economy Fitted by a Model of Additive Preferences', *Econometrica* (1966).

[51] M. Richter, 'Revealed Preference Theory', *Econometrica* (1966).

[52] P. Samuelson, 'A Note on the Pure Theory of Consumer Behaviour', *Economica* (1938).

[53] P. Samuelson, *Foundations of Economic Analysis* (Cambridge, Mass.: Harvard University Press, 1947).

[54] D. Schmeidler, 'A Condition for the Completeness of Partial Preference Relations', *Econometrica* (1971).

[55] R. Shephard, *Cost and Production Functions* (Princeton, N.J.: Princeton University Press, 1953).

[56] E. Slutsky, 'On the Theory of the Budget of the Consumer', translated from Italian in *Readings in Price Theory*, ed. K. Boulding and G. Stigler (Allen & Unwin, 1953).

[57] H. Sonnenschein, 'The Relationship between Transitive Preference and the Structure of the Choice Space', *Econometrica* (1965).

[58] R. Stone, *Mathematical Models of the Economy and other Essays* (Chapman & Hall, 1970).

[59] R. Strotz, 'The Utility Tree', *Econometrica* (1958).

[60] H. Uzawa, 'Preference and Rational Choice in the Theory of Consumption', in *Mathematical Methods in the Social Sciences*, ed. K. Arrow, S. Karlin and P. Suppes (Stanford: Stanford University Press, 1960).

[61] T. Yokoyama, 'A Logical Foundation of the Theory of Consumer Demand', *Osaka Economic Papers* (1953).

[62] H. Wold and L. Jureen, *Demand Analysis* (New York: Wiley, 1953).

Index